Conte

Thank You, Teacher

Thank you, teacher, for making a difference! This uplifting book by motivational speakers Brad Johnson and Hal Bowman provides daily encouragement to keep you feeling inspired on your educational journey. It features 100 letters, written by teachers across the country and addressed to YOU. The letters highlight topics such as celebrating small successes, bringing out the best in your students, and knowing your worth. The book is perfect for teachers of all grade levels, and for principals to buy their teachers for schoolwide morale. Read one letter each morning to kick off your day, or use them to launch staff meetings or PD days. The comforting, affirming advice will remind you why you've chosen this profession, that you're not alone, that you can get through your toughest days, and that you're having a big impact!

Brad Johnson (@DrBradJohnson) has 25 years of experience as a teacher and administrator at the K–12 and collegiate level. He is a national speaker and author focusing on servant leadership and teacher advocacy.

Hal Bowman (@halbowman) is a renowned speaker, education consultant, and the creator of transformational programs like *Teach Like a Rock Star* and *Be the One*. Before becoming a full-time speaker, he spent over 20 years in K–12 classrooms, teaching everything from Band to Biology.

Also Available from Routledge Eye On Education

Dear Teacher:
100 Days of Inspirational Quotes and Anecdotes
Brad Johnson and Hal Bowman

Principal Bootcamp:
Accelerated Strategies to Influence and Lead from Day One
Brad Johnson

Putting Teachers First:
How to Inspire, Motivate, and Connect with Your Staff
Brad Johnson

Learning On Your Feet, 2e:
Incorporating Physical Activity into the K-8 Classroom
Brad Johnson and Melody Jones

What Schools Don't Teach:
20 Ways to Help Students Excel in School and in Life
Brad Johnson and Julie Sessions

From School Administrator to School Leader:
15 Keys to Maximizing Your Leadership Potential
Brad Johnson and Julie Sessions

Thank You, Teacher

100 Uplifting and Affirming Letters from Your Fellow Educators

Brad Johnson and Hal Bowman

Routledge
Taylor & Francis Group

NEW YORK AND LONDON

Cover image: © Getty Images

First published 2022
by Routledge
605 Third Avenue, New York, NY 10158

and by Routledge
4 Park Square, Milton Park, Abingdon, Oxon, OX14 4RN

Routledge is an imprint of the Taylor & Francis Group, an informa business

Library of Congress Cataloging-in-Publication Data
Names: Johnson, Brad, 1969– author. | Bowman, Hal, author.
Title: Thank you, teacher! : 100 uplifting and affirming letters from your fellow educators / Brad Johnson and Hal Bowman.
Other titles: One hundred uplifting and affirming letters from your fellow educators
Description: First Edition. | New York : Routledge, 2022.
Identifiers: LCCN 2021051420 (print) | LCCN 2021051421 (ebook) | ISBN 9781032107745 (Hardback) | ISBN 9781032068299 (Paperback) | ISBN 9781003216988 (eBook)
Subjects: LCSH: Teachers–Conduct of life. | Motivation in education.
Classification: LCC LB1775 .J5457 2022 (print) |
LCC LB1775 (ebook) | DDC 371.1–dc23/eng/20220211
LC record available at https://lccn.loc.gov/2021051420
LC ebook record available at https://lccn.loc.gov/2021051421

ISBN: 978-1-032-10774-5 (hbk)
ISBN: 978-1-032-06829-9 (pbk)
ISBN: 978-1-003-21698-8 (ebk)

DOI: 10.4324/9781003216988

Typeset in Palatino LT Std
by Newgen Publishing UK

Meet the Authors

Dr. Brad Johnson is one of the most dynamic and engaging speakers in the fields of education and leadership. He has 25 years of experience in the trenches as a teacher and administrator. Dr. Johnson is transforming how teachers lead in the classroom and how administrators lead in the school. He is a servant leader who shares his vast experiences and expertise to help other educators maximize their potential. He is the author of many books, including *Principal Bootcamp, Putting Teachers First*, and *Learning on Your Feet*. He has traveled the globe speaking and training teachers and educational leaders.

After 20 years in the classroom, **Hal Bowman** has spent the last decade inspiring hundreds of thousands of educators, delivering effective tools and strategies that transform classroom and campus culture. He is the creator of four unique programs: *Teach Like a Rock Star, Hal Bowman's Be The One, Change a Kid's Life*, and *Shout it From the Rooftops*. Onstage, Hal's high-powered, lively keynotes and events have revolutionized professional development in education, offering a refreshing approach that inspires teachers to reconnect with their passion for changing their students' lives in profound and meaningful ways. Online, Hal reaches countless educators each week as the host of the Teach *Like A Rock Star Podcast* and *Help a Teacher Facebook Live with Hal Bowman*. He is also the founder of *Men in Education*, an online platform for educators providing community, personal growth, and professional development addressing the unique roles men can play in the lives of students. Hal has committed his life to keeping his finger on the ever-changing pulse of education in America. He lives happily in Houston, Texas with his wife and two kids. He also shares his home with a few furry four-legged creatures who are not moved, in the least, by his inspirational prowess.

Preface

Doc Brad and I spend a lot of time on the road speaking to educators at conferences and schools across the nation. In fact, every year during the month of August – as schools are gearing up to launch into the new school year – we pretty much spend the entire four weeks either on a stage, on a plane, in a rental car, or in a hotel room.

This year, as we were recovering from traveling to all of our back-to-school August events, Doc Brad and I were talking about our experiences with the educators we met across the country. As we were exchanging notes and swapping stories, we realized that we kept coming back to the same common theme: Never before have we been more impressed, amazed, and proud of the heroic work that teachers are doing in their classrooms!

What we witnessed in schools across the nation was truly astounding.

As teaching has become increasingly more difficult – more kids with less instructional time, greater expectations with less direction, more accountability with less resources, more rigorous curriculum mandated for students (many of who are years behind), all while taking care of the emotional needs of children in the middle of a pandemic – educators have responded by becoming more creative, more resourceful, and more committed to being a positive, influential force in the lives of their students. It's incredible to see how millions of educators, despite the monumental challenges, are continuing to use the content of their classrooms to create high-performing kids of exceptional character. And it's not like we saw this kind of remarkable effort occasionally. We saw it consistently at every single school we visited.

As we chatted and marveled over the Herculean effort of teachers, we wondered, "How could we possibly thank educators in a meaningful way for their valiant, unwavering commitment to their students? How could we possibly articulate our appreciation?" We quickly realized that, rather than us, the people most qualified to express the most sincere, deepest gratitude of all are those who truly understand the role of an educator – teachers themselves.

So, we began by asking a handful of teachers one simple request: "Would you be willing to write a thank you note to educators?"

The response was overwhelming! We didn't just receive thank you notes. We received beautifully written, emotional letters that spoke from the heart of one teacher directly to the hearts of all teachers.

Please keep in mind that this book is filled with letters of appreciation written by real educators. These are not your social media superstar edu-gurus with their perfectly filtered, Pinterest-ready photos of their perfect outfits in their perfect classrooms with their perfect lesson plans perfectly designed and perfectly delivered to their perfect students where every day is the perfect day. Instead, these letters are written by real, everyday, ordinary teachers who are producing extraordinary results with their kids. These are teachers just like you and I. The kind of teacher who struggles; often feels isolated; second guesses just about everything, everyday; regularly feels like they're not doing enough; constantly worries about their students; cries in their car before heading home; yet wakes up the next day, drinks a gallon of coffee, and steps into the classroom ready, willing, and excited to teach and love their kids relentlessly.

You'll notice that we have included a handful of letters from some educators who are not in the classroom. They are district leaders, campus administrators, retired educators, and even a principal's secretary. I can assure you that these people truly are teachers in every way. They may have a different title, but they share the same role and commitment as you and I: change a kid's life. When you read their letters, you'll see what I mean. Their dedication and passion for making a difference for kids is obvious.

Finally, before you start turning the pages that follow, know that it's not just those people who contributed letters to this book who are filled with appreciation for all that you do for your students, it's all of us – everyone, everywhere, and especially Doc Brad and myself.

We see you.
We applaud you.
We are proud of you.
We appreciate you.
We love you.

Beyond Compliance

1

Dear Teacher,

I begin my letter to you with the following quote to reflect on:

> *"Some of the most brilliant, creative people I know did not do well at school. Many of them didn't really discover what they could do—and who they really were—until they'd left school and recovered from their education." – Sir Ken Robinson*

Those last four words of Sir Ken Robinson's quote are haunting, but an important truth to remember. The fact is, as an adult, a teacher holds an unbelievable amount of power to yield a negative or positive impact on a child's life. We have the capacity to serve students as much more than a facilitator of learning experiences. It is within our power to create a classroom culture that fosters a sense of community and respect, recognizing the inherent value of each member. It is within our power to infuse joy and creativity into learning. It is within our power to recognize and honor the unique background and culture of every student.

In the spirit of Robinson's quote, I challenge you to be the antecedent to a student feeling unaware and unrecognized of their brilliance and creativity, and ultimately their potential. This is more important than any singular focus on curriculum, pacing guide, or learning outcome. This places the student, every student, above any learning number or statistic that can be attached to their identity. It asks you to see every student for who they are, not what you want them to be. Too often in the name of conformity and management, we apply systems and practices in our daily routines at school to make things easier, but do nothing to recognize and further develop the unique qualities or endeavors of our students. We should desire more from our students than compliance. We should value self-direction and foster personalized learning experiences, giving students the

DOI: 10.4324/9781003216988-1

opportunity to develop important skills, as well as adding to their enjoyment and engagement.

Here are some simple strategies to strengthen classroom connection and inspire joyful learning:

- ◆ Adopt a design-thinking mindset where trial and error are simply part of the learning process and promote innovation and creativity
- ◆ Allow student-partnerships
- ◆ Develop students as self-assessors and don't grade everything
- ◆ Encourage students to show their learning in a way that is meaningful to them
- ◆ Facilitate skill building opportunities for students to evaluate peers and offer specific feedback for improvement
- ◆ Infuse lessons with opportunities for student-led exploration of the topic
- ◆ Use reflection as a routine process of instruction and learning

As teachers, we have this amazing opportunity to share in the lives of young people. Those individuals deserve a teacher who will champion them, honor them, and prepare them for the future. When we create a culture that invites student creativity, autonomy, and inquiry over compliance, we support a rich, diverse, inclusive environment where a love of learning dominates and every student KNOWS they belong.

I commend you, my fellow teacher, for the work you do. Thank you for sharing your gifts and expertise with young people.

Most Sincerely,

Abigail French
2020 ASCD Emerging Leader
Seventh Grade U.S. History Teacher
Frederick County Middle School
Winchester, Virginia

You Are Worth It

2

Dear Teacher,

Don't forget.

Don't forget to take care of you. Doing this is hard for so many because we all became educators for various reasons, but those reasons typically all center around one focus—*our students*. Because of this, we spend most of our time taking care of others before ever considering the importance of taking care of ourselves. For years, I thought the stress and anxiety that I felt each year was normal and just a part of being an educator. It took me a long time to recognize that I was taking care of everyone but myself. I am still a work in progress, but each day I am working towards taking care of me. Your self-care is personal to you. You might not find it in books or blogs or hear it in a podcast, because it's personal to you. There isn't a prescription for self-care.

What brings your peace? What calms your anxiety and fears? What makes you happy?

This will look different for EVERYONE. Once again, there is not a prescribed way to self-care. You can find support and advice, but ultimately the "self" in self-care will prevail.

Don't forget.

You are worth it.

Amy Storer
Educator and Learner
Plantersville, Texas

DOI: 10.4324/9781003216988-2

Permission to Shine

3

Dear Teacher,

You are my hero! Day in and day out, you courageously step into an arena that is changing lives and changing history. Daily you stare into the faces of adversity and security, difference and indifference, passion and aggression, fear and confidence, chaos and calm, hate and love. I want you to know that you are seen!

My dear friend, where to begin? In the words of Brené Brown, "You are working on the hardest edges of love." THAT'S HARD my person! This world can be full of woe… RUN THE OTHER WAY!!

Crucial to thriving, not simply surviving, is relationships. Surround yourself with people who will war for you, collaborate with you, and make you belly laugh. Your students see and absorb more than you will ever know. Modeling relationships that grow you and refine you far outreaches your life. You know, the ripple effect. We are all built for connection and you deserve to be connected with the people who will deposit into you daily, including a mentor. Regardless of your years on this journey, find a person who leads with integrity that you can emulate, holds you accountable to your WHY, and pushes you to YOUR fullest and greatest potential. AND LAUGHS WITH YOU!

I taught middle school/high school English Language Arts and Reading for 15 years. Several years ago, I was studying about confidence and motivation (Ok. I was really watching "Coach Carter") and decided to try a little experiment on myself and my students. I saw the character of Cruz in several of my students and was struggling to break down the walls. So, we memorized Marianne Willamson's poem, "Our Deepest Fear," together. We didn't just memorize it though. We studied it. We studied ourselves. I began to see students who barely came to class show up and show out – in a good way. I saw students helping students

DOI: 10.4324/9781003216988-3

without my prompting and friendships form between students who never would've crossed "the tracks," if you get my drift.

Your light transfers to those around you. I give you permission! Get outside your comfort zone. Be vulnerable with your students. If you want them to become GREAT, YOU have to show them what that looks like, sounds like, and feels like. Some of your students have never truly experienced authenticity with an adult without judgment. Craziest thing happened, I learned things about myself that were buried deep down inside. That freedom led to a realization that previously I taught out of a place of control, not confidence. From a place of correction, not contribution. Flip the script on yourself, I dare you. I double-dog dare you!

My final thought, for now, is stay connected to your WHY. When that becomes blurry, so does everything else. Several years into teaching, my WHY was more like looking through a kaleidoscope than a telescope. I took a two-year sabbatical and found a new mentor, yes I did! In redefining my WHY, I learned how to say, "NO." (Probably the most power-packed two letters in the English language!) I learned that boundaries are good and necessary. You do not have to be, nor can you be, all things to all people. Your WHY can shift, just make sure it's clear. We all have strengths and weaknesses. Focus on the first and later they will become future stepping stones.

Even though I do not know you, my admiration for you runs deep. YOU are leading the future of our tomorrows. YOU are "powerful beyond measure."

Let YOUR light shine!

Angi Thomas
Special Education Behavior Consultant
Abilene, Texas

Focus on your strengths.

Infinitely Different Days 4

Dear Teacher,

I am wondering what kind of day you've had as you sit down to read this letter. There are so many ways a teacher's day can go. It helps me to know we share all these kinds of days. Maybe it will help you.

Perhaps it was a sad day. A day when one of your kids doesn't show up because they suddenly moved away and you didn't get to send them off with a loving farewell. You'll miss them and you're afraid they won't have any idea. Know that your love for that child is part of them now and goes with them. It stays with you at the same time. Feel it all.

Did this day make you proud? Maybe some of your kids were thrilled with a story you shared, mastered an algorithm, achieved the next reading level, managed a conflict in a healthy way, were kind to each other. These days remind us why we keep showing up. Let that pride fill your heart.

Maybe this one was a day that brought you to the kind of anger that shakes your hands and tangles your guts. A day when you feel pressure to make progress and the students have anything but that on their minds. Playing, flirting, talking, talking, TALKING regardless of your carefully managed routines and cherished relationships. You are not alone. It's a day that requires deep breathing and reminding yourself to remember the fact that these behaviors, too, need practice if these young humans are going to grow well, whether or not it's on our own agenda. Breathe. Know you have plenty of company and tomorrow will be another day, a different day.

Was today a happy day? One in which you felt like the moderator of a model United Nations meeting, everyone happily working together toward a common purpose, concentrating on the task at hand? Soak this day up and let your pleasure fill your

DOI: 10.4324/9781003216988-4

body right out through the ends of your fingers and toes. Let it fortify you.

Some days are frustrating days. The kind of day with meetings in which it is stated that the growth your students have made is simply not enough, when interruptions and pullouts kept distracting you and your class from the hard work needing to be done. Another good day to breathe deeply, let yourself gaze on these small people and realize your immense privilege in creating a space for them to grow and thrive in your care, at their own pace.

Maybe it was a funny day. Did one of your strugglers purposefully change the text of an article to support his wish for vampires to be real? This happened to me and the memory of my laughter and his indignance still makes me chuckle. Times like these are worth writing down to sustain you later. Kids can be so funny.

Our teaching brings about infinitely different days. We are never bored or complacent. We remember why we teach, know that we are enough and that we make a difference, appreciate the privilege of working with young people who need us. Don't forget to go mindfully through your days, however they go. No two of our days will ever be just alike. Not all professionals get to say that.

With love,

Anne Armstrong
Elementary Educator
Plano, Texas

Warriors

5

Dear Teacher,

You, my friend, are a Warrior.

Each day you battle the seen and unseen, and failure is not an option.

You don your selectively permeable armor each morning. A breastplate covers your heart, but you remove it, knowing that the love that lives there will far outweigh the pain of sympathizing with your students' struggles. The armor's purpose is not to protect you, but to safeguard your students from your own conflicted emotions. It projects positivity and light. It smiles a thousand genuine smiles. It provides you the flexibility to stand in strength when advocating for your students yet bow down to tie a shoe of a small child. It allows you to be exactly who your students need you to be.

Flanked by Maslov and Bloom, you wield your sword of knowledge with passion, imparting wisdom upon your students. You rescue those in your charge from hunger, homelessness, addiction, abuse, incarceration, divorce, and emotional and economic poverty, even if just for a few hours. You cut through life's distractions to deliver engaging lessons. Your battle plan requires you to differentiate, guide, assess, enrich, modify, intervene, and accommodate simultaneously and at a moment's notice. You create, motivate, and inspire. You meet the needs of your students whether they are physical, emotional, social, or academic. You are your students' hero.

Your precious Warrior heart is infinitely brave. It surpasses the emotional depth of any other. It converts your own pain and sadness to authentically perfect compassion. It exudes patience and understanding and extends mercy and grace. It moves you to instill good character, cultivate self-efficacy, and assure students of their worthiness, not for how they perform, but simply for being present. You celebrate accomplishments, dry tears, and

DOI: 10.4324/9781003216988-5

build relationships on your best days… and your worst. You are your students' champion.

You approach every battle with humility and through the lens of empathy and compassion. You never lose hope and you never lose faith. You refuse to give up on any student or in your quest to empower your students to be their best selves. The Hunkpapa Lakota leader Sitting Bull defined a warrior not as a fighter, but as one who sacrifices oneself for others. He tasked a warrior with caring for "the defenseless, those who cannot provide for themselves, and above all, the children, the future of humanity."

You, my friend, are a Warrior, and I am honored to walk among your ranks.

Respectfully,

Ashley Evans
School Counselor
Caney, Kansas

Taking Back ENOUGH! 6

Dear Teacher,

Enough.

It's a word that weighs heavily on the hearts of every single educator I know. One word that carries a LOT of weight. *Enough.* There's never enough time. There's never *enough* money. Sometimes we're even told we're not doing *enough*. We didn't document *enough*. We didn't collect *enough* data. We don't have *enough* resources. There's not *enough* parental involvement. Our students didn't make *enough* progress. The list of "never *enough*" goes on and on.

Teacher have heard it time and time again. We've heard it so much from so many different sources… administration, instructional coaches, parents, co-workers, and sometimes it comes right out of our own mouths. *Enough, enough, enough*… I don't know about you, but – for me – it doesn't even sound like a word sometimes. Just a mumble covered in a tone of failure that's always sitting in the back of our minds. It can be overwhelming and can cause the confidence of the most capable and caring teachers to crumble. That just doesn't sit right with me. So, guess what, teacher…

Enough is enough. You don't have to let the negative connotation overtake your classroom. This job is hard *enough*. There's so much weight without the added pressure of *enough*. So, it's time for you to take back that word. It's time to take "enough" back. I know you're wondering how you can do that. We can't change the fact that there's not *enough* time, or money, or resources. I'll tell you how. I'll tell you what you need to remember.

YOU. ARE. ENOUGH. Those kids, YOUR kids, are so lucky to have someone who loves them ENOUGH to make sacrifices every single day. You love your kids ENOUGH. You care ENOUGH. You are doing ENOUGH. Even on the days where all you feel like you did was show up and make your kids smile…

DOI: 10.4324/9781003216988-6

that was ENOUGH. Maybe you didn't decorate your room like the teacher next door. Maybe you didn't meet the goals that were picked out for you. Maybe it feels like every other teacher around you is sprinting and you are just barely crawling. Don't compare another teacher's "enough" with your "enough." If you love your job and love those students, *YOUR* enough *IS* enough. Every day that you show up and put a smile on your face and change a kid's life. Well, teacher… that is MORE than *enough*.

We are ALL enough,

Mrs. Bethani Franklin
Kindergarten Teacher
Franklinton, Louisiana

Dear Cassidy

7

The following letter was written by Dr. Rob Carroll to his daughter, Cassidy Carroll, on the eve of her first day of teaching. The letter that follows was written by Cassidy during her third year as a teacher.

Dear Cassidy,

I know as you try to sleep tonight that you will be this excited terrified mix of emotions. I want you to set your alarm… give yourself plenty of time of course… but close your eyes with certainty and peace about the choice that you made. You were born to teach. There is no doubt. I saw it before you went to school. I saw it every day that you danced down to class. I saw it in how you made friends with all your classmates! I saw it in how you always were passionate about the "underdog!" I saw it in your incredible school spirit and I saw it in your understanding of what great teaching is all about.

In the morning, when you wake up and put on some super cute outfit and do your hair just right… I want to share with you some truths that I believe may be of help. Here they are:

- You have unlimited potential within you… so much it blows my mind but potential is not enough… you have to work hard and believe in yourself every day!
- I love that you are charting your course in your own school and in your own district! There I will be known as Cassidy's dad and that's all I want to be!
- Always remember that teaching is not about you or your content… those are both important but teaching is about all those beautiful individuals in your classes everyday!

DOI: 10.4324/9781003216988-7

◆ You are a <u>member</u> of a team! <u>Be the type of team member that they can look up to… that they can depend on!</u>

◆ Through your teaching flows bits and pieces of many great people… many that you know and some you did not. You are a collection of every experience you ever had. You have bits of Pa, Ma, Duckworth, Guess, Butzin, Smith, Kopshever, Estabrook, Dixon, Long, and even Keating (from Dead Poet's Society) just to name a few!

◆ Make no excuses! They are for losers and you are not a loser!

◆ Don't ever scale back your teaching, your enthusiasm, your love of your career so that someone does not need to improve theirs!

◆ Eat with your kids every once in while… many times it's overlooked but oh so important!

◆ You will cry… maybe today… maybe tomorrow… that's ok. That means you are human!

◆ Reflect at the end of every day on your ride home! Start with what you did well and then think about how you can do better! If you do this every day… you will never get stale and you will always grow!

◆ You are a badass… always remember that! You can handle anything! You are Cassidy Halen Carroll!

Finally, remember that I love you! You are my first princess and that is something that time nor miles between us can ever change! Now, get in your Hyundai, turn up Van Halen, and go change the world!

Daddy

Dr. Rob Carroll
Assistant Professor
University of Southern Indiana

Creating Hope

8

Dear Teacher,

I see you. I see the passion that flows through your veins, no matter how subdued. I see the worry that creates lines in the soft skin around your eyes as you lay your head down at night. I see the glimmer in your eyes as important connections are made with a student that really needs it... I know you are imagining that student right now. I see you.

But others in this world... they don't always see you. The people that reside outside the home base of a school building don't see the family that was born within those cinder block walls. They don't see the hours that you spend outside of the school day making sure that your content is perfect. They don't see the food that you bring for a child that does not have it at home. They don't see you fighting for a classroom full of equity and hope. They may not see it... so they do not fully understand what it means to be a teacher. The outside world has a way of damaging a teacher's very core: their passion. The feeling of being unseen can seep through your morning coffee; it can steal your moments of joy. I have sat in this feeling too. Let me explain.

I never wanted to be a teacher... I wanted to pursue a profession in veterinary science, marine biology, geology, or even a really cool businesswoman. I wanted to change the world and make it a better place to live. Teaching was never on my radar. I grew up in a school; my dad was the best of the best in education. He led a struggling school to nationwide success in a matter of a career. He never pushed me to be a teacher because he knew that a person must be called to this profession. As I entered my senior year of high school, I began seeing the world in a different light... a more realistic light. Because of my education and growing critical thinking skills, events in the world led me to start thinking of new dreams. Climate problems created tragic situations for the country, students began feeling unsafe at school, and inequality

DOI: 10.4324/9781003216988-8

was speaking up. As a senior in high school, I knew this was my generation's time to change the course of history. I knew that I had been called to educate and inspire the coming generation. My idea of changing the world shifted and my career aspirations followed suit. I became a teacher.

On my first day of school at my very first teaching job, I received a letter from my dad that has stuck with me to this day. This letter helped sustain me through the highs and lows that I have experienced in this profession. He encouraged me to never scale back my teaching passion just so someone else will feel better about theirs. He told me to make no excuses about my students' success. He told me to remember the great teachers that had come before me. But most importantly, he told me to reflect at the end of each day.

I was full of passion when I entered teaching. My motto has always been to create world changers in my classroom. But as my first years of teaching progressed, I realized that the passion of the job could not sustain me. The outside world does not always see the care that is put into school decisions and often the national conversation regarding schools can become negative. I became lost in the voices that were doubting teacher effectiveness and ability to create successful humans. My drive home from work became a time to feel sad about the passion I was losing.

But then, I remembered the letter that was written to me by a very special educator, my dad. *Reflect*. And so, I reflected. I reflected on my abilities, on my hopes for my students, and on my hopes for this profession. I reflected on the things that I could do to make my school a better, more equitable place. I reflected on my career and in doing so, I want to add one more piece of advice to my dad's letter.

Always reflect on the hope that you have for your students, your profession, and yourself.

Teachers have the ability to change the trajectory of the next generation because of the hope that they provide in the classroom. Teachers have the ability to impart wisdom, ethics, and morality onto their students when the world outside their classroom door seems to leave these qualities behind. Our students look to us, teachers, when the world outside of the classroom creates injustice, inequity, and a loss of love. It is our job to instill in them the hope that we have for their future. The hope that we have for the betterment of our world.

When you feel like the outside world does not see you, remember the young eyes that see you every day. Reflect on the hope that you have for these humans. Reflect on the hope that you have for this profession. As you move forward in your career, write down your hope for future generations. What do you wish the world would look like? What do you hope our students see as they get older? What do you hope our students will become? This hope... even if on one little sticky note, will be everything you need when the present world seems to get in our profession's way. Reflect on this hope Every. Single. Day.

And when you come in the next day, fight. Fight for the hope that you feel. Advocate for a better world for your students. Advocate for a better environment for your school. Let your reflection of hope decide your trajectory. Be the hope. Share hope. Be a teacher.

 You got this,
Cassidy

Cassidy Carroll
7th Grade ELA Teacher
Henderson, Kentucky

Never Forget 9

Dear Teacher,

Today you want to quit. Today you think to yourself that you are in the wrong profession. You are frustrated, disappointed, and tired. Maybe you could sell insurance or manage an Old Navy… Why not? How easy that would be! You wonder if what you are doing is making any difference at all.

Just as you are formulating an exit plan, you start to think about the students you would be leaving behind. You think about the students that you know better than anyone. You reflect on how much time it took you to get that one shy student to finally speak to you. You remember how the one student with the hair in his eye always smiles back with such excitement when he sees you smile first, as if it is the only smile he sees in a day.

You smile about that one day when every student seemed to be engaged for the entire lesson and everything went well. You get a bit emotional thinking about the time that the girl in the second row stayed after class to tell you that her parents were splitting up and how she was sad to move. You laugh out loud when you get a flash of the time when your class clown somehow kicked his foot so hard his shoe flew up and damaged the ceiling tile. You were so mad that day. Now, all you really remember is the remorse he showed and how he volunteered to stay after school to help clean up and repair the ceiling.

Finally, you realize something important. It hits you like a freight train. You really do not have to worry about whether you are making a difference in students' lives, in the community, or even in the world. The role of a teacher inherently impacts. You make a difference in every student's life that you have the privilege of serving. As a teacher, you never get to decide if this calling is an important one or if you make a difference in your students' lives. You ONLY get to decide what kind of difference you will make.

DOI: 10.4324/9781003216988-9

Today you want to be a teacher all over again. You realize that there is no greater profession. You know that it takes a special person to return day after day and year after year, but you feel so blessed to be able to be that person. You are inspired, motivated, and re-energized. How sad it would be to have a job that doesn't really matter! You are so glad that you are doing something that makes all the difference in the world.

Today and every day you are a teacher. May all teachers never forget what that means.

Courtney Sharkey

"Teacher for Life"
Richardson, Texas

When You Know Better, Do Better

Dear Teacher,

I began my teaching career in 1999 when everything seemed so right with the world. At 22 years old, in my little corner in Ohio, I felt like I was on top of the world. I was making $28,000 as a first year English/theatre teacher and theatre director. I had my own little apartment and a late model used car. I was single with no kids. I went to work every day at a great suburban high school and taught to the best of my ability. The kids loved me, I loved the kids, I loved my school, job, and life. A year later, I began working on my Master's degree in Educational Leadership and Supervision. My horizons began to expand. Although I was young, I began to reflect more and think about when things were not right with the world; more specifically, when I was a little black girl growing up in a predominantly white suburban area in the 1980s.

As I reflect on the inequities in education from the 1980s, I think that we may have simply thought "That's just how it is." For example, I was placed in a low-level reading group despite being able to read when I entered Kindergarten. Being one of the few Black kids in the class, it wasn't until I got older that I questioned the exclusion that I faced when it was time for Reading groups. I suppose my parents thought, "That's just how it is."

In 1st grade, I received a "swat,"/paddling from the principal because I was accused by a white student of stealing clay. I told the teacher, principal, and my parents that this was not true; but I specifically remember my parents getting dressed up to meet the principal on the evening of the paddling and being present as the Principal carried through with the punishment.

DOI: 10.4324/9781003216988-10

I suppose "That's just how it was!" and my parents accepted the outcome with little disagreement.

Maya Angelou once said, "Then when you know better, do better." As I look back over my teaching career one thing I wish I would have focused on in my early years was the equity and equality of my students. These two words have recently become buzz words but their value and placement in society have always been there.

As I moved through my career, I would look back and jokingly say "I'm sorry to my previous students" because I did not know any better. While I can definitely give myself some grace and say that I was a quality teacher with excellent evaluations to match, I could have done better and been deemed an amazing teacher!

Reflecting on my teaching experiences, here are some things I could have done better to achieve that:

1. I could have taken more time to reflect on my practices and worked more to enhance personalized learning. You see, "back in my day," (the late 90's), my reflection was a self-created checklist which consisted of standards such as: "Did the students like the lesson?" "Did the students learn the intended goal?" and "What will I change about this lesson for in the future?" Reflecting back on this now, I would have made the questions more individualized and focused on students' personal needs and outcomes as opposed to looking at the lesson as a whole. While I was well aware of students with unique abilities and the necessary modifications and accommodations, oftentimes I would limit these modifications and accommodations to just students on IEPs; the remainder of my students were simply expected to keep working and seek me out for any additional guidance and support.

2. I could have read more and learned about additional strategies that would have had a greater impact on my students from diverse backgrounds. Although the research, information, and support is nowhere near what it is now, there were definitely resources that I could have

sought to help my English language learners, students of color, and students in poverty.

3. I could have had a more impactful role on my school as a whole. I was honored to create Black History Month displays and serve on small committees for Diversity Programs but unfortunately, I did not challenge the school to look at policies and practices that could change the atmosphere for the Black students, for example.

When you know better, do better! As I reflect back on my career, it kinda makes me sad to think of how my students talked about how great I was and still sing my praises to this day but I think I was quite mediocre based on today's standards. We are all learners, despite being teachers.

Teacher, here are some important reminders:

◆ Take time to time to reflect on your own personal and professional experiences.
◆ Learn and grow.
◆ Look at and celebrate the ties that bind us as well as our unique differences that make us special.
◆ Recognize systemic racism and how it still affects students today.
◆ Make an impact on your school as a whole.

You got this! Now, go be the greatness that I thought I was.

Dr. Kristilynn Turney
CEO/Founder of Dr. Kristilynn Turney, LLC and EdPD, LLC
Cincinnati, Ohio

You Are Enough!

11

Dear Teacher,

In case you were wondering, you are enough. You do not need to try every new strategy, read every new book or listen to every new podcast to be what you need for your students. Students will remember what you teach them because of WHO YOU ARE. This is what teaching from the heart is all about. It's about the BEING more than the DOING. Adults ask students what they want to BE when they grow up, not what they want to do. As adults we shift the focus from being to doing and that is when we feel like we are not enough. But you are enough. When you feel like you are not doing enough, pause and remind yourself of the BEING rather than the doing.

How do we remind ourselves? We remember what it feels like to BE a teacher. We sometimes get stuck in doing the things that a teacher does, so we need to sit back and remember how it FEELS. You know. Engage your senses in the feeling. What does being a teacher look like, sound like, feel like, and even smell and sometimes taste like (we all know the taste of school lunches, right?). You know when you are teaching from the heart. It's when you get so excited and lose track of time and then you hear the bell ring. It's when you can feel goosebumps on your skin when you see that child that has never raised their hand all year finally raise it high. It's when you feel the buzz in the classroom when kids are discussing, collaborating and connecting and you walk around smiling, soaking it all in. It's that first day of school, freshly sharpened pencil smell – every year – feeling. It's the feeling you had when you walked in your first classroom and saw a student smile at you and say hello. You have that teacher feeling inside you and you just need to take a moment, pause and remember. Think, right now of those moments and hang onto them. They are right there in your mind whenever you need them. You are enough.

DOI: 10.4324/9781003216988-11

You are enough when you are BEING YOU for your students. Think about your talents, skills, passions and loves. All of those are what YOU bring to your classroom every day. They will remember the "you being you" part of teaching the most, and you bring it every day! How? It is when you are being present listening to a child talk about their favorite movie, when you are cheering them on in a game, when you act goofy to get them to smile, when you say hi and welcome them to class, and when you are simply BEING YOU. They learn and connect to you because of who you are when you are BEING you. You are enough.

Think about it this way. Remember a time when you learned something new because of a positive experience you had. Yes, the mechanics, facts, modeling and practice were important, but think about what you remember most about those moments. How did you feel? Who was that supportive person that was teaching you? We know the statistic that teachers are THE most important factor in student learning. Did you hear that – the teacher, not the content. Our successful learning experiences are because of the person: the content is the same but the people being themselves and bringing their unique traits to the learning are what made it stick. You are enough.

Now think about your classroom. You set the tone and create that experience with the content you teach just by BEING YOU. You are the leader in your classroom and your students thank you for bringing the passion, ideas, expertise, stories and fun to your content. More than all that though, your students thank you when you are BEING more than doing. You are forever leaving a lasting impression on them and are modeling for them the importance of BEING themselves in the learning process. You are enough.

Thank you for BEING YOU,

Dr. Toni Hull,
Executive Director of Curriculum & Instructional Innovation,
Hatch, New Mexico

Just One

Dear Teacher,

I know you are tired. I know there are very few people, if any, in your family who truly understand what you do every day. I am sure there are times you have questioned your decision to become a teacher, but I want you to know that what you are doing for kids is worth it. Even on days when you feel like you aren't making a difference, I assure you, you are making a lasting impression.

There are students who have or will come through your classroom who you notice right away need you. Their clothes are dirty, their shoes don't fit, and they crave the love you have to give. You pour all of your resources into these students to make a difference in their lives. Others will be just as obviously needy, but they refuse to accept your love and guidance; yet you work tirelessly to tear down their walls of pain so you can reach them. Some of your students have such disruptive behaviors that you can't help but give them your undivided attention. You have researched behavior management topics for hours in an attempt to get their behavior under control. There is no doubt these students need you, and you make a difference in their lives.

Then there's the student whose needs are not so obvious. The student who rides the bus to school every day, has clean clothes, is well behaved and mannerly. This student appears to be an average student, completing assignments, making good grades, maintaining perfect attendance, and never disrespectful. This student is not even on your radar as being needy; however, when you take the time to think about this student, you may realize she only participates in class when called upon but doesn't offer anything to discussions voluntarily. As you learn more about the student, you may wonder why this student who appears to come from a stable middle-class family isn't involved in any school-related activities. With questioning and observation, you may

DOI: 10.4324/9781003216988-12

be shocked to learn this is the same student who seems to be well-liked, but she escapes to the library during lunch to avoid the cafeteria crowd. Yes, this is a student who also needs you. In my opinion, these students often fall through the cracks because they have become masters at blending in just enough so as not to call attention to themselves.

So, you might be asking yourself, "What does a student like this need?" or "What do I have to offer students like this?" In my experience, these are the students who simply need *you*: your time, attention, and conversation. There are many approaches that work with this type of student. For example, there's a strategy called the "2 × 10" that encourages you to spend two minutes a day with this student individually for ten consecutive school days talking about anything except school-related topics. By doing something like this, you might learn that the student isn't involved in school-related activities because her mother works late, and there is no one to pick her up after the activities, but she has a strong desire to participate. She hasn't even mentioned to her mother that she has an interest in after school activities because she knows what a hardship it would put on her mother to try to pick her up. You might learn that both of her parents are educated, but they divorced when she was very young, and she is being raised by a single parent. You could possibly find out that her oldest brother has been in the hospital for almost a year due to a terrible motorcycle accident, so money is scarce; she doesn't eat in the cafeteria because she doesn't want anyone to know she doesn't have lunch money or has only a mayonnaise sandwich for lunch. As a teacher, when you know these types of things about your students, you can really spring into action and find a way to meet those needs. I have never come across a teacher in my career who wouldn't find a way to help this student if they knew the student's situation. I firmly believe that one significant adult at school can change a student's life and redirect her path, and I hope you commit to being that significant adult.

In closing, I want to emphasize to you the important influence you have as a teacher. I want to encourage you to get to know your students, those who have hidden needs as well as those who have obvious needs. Finally, I urge you to communicate with your students; spend time with them talking about things other than school. You might be the one to change the path of a future high school dropout or teen mother. You could be teaching the first high school or college graduate in a family. I know you are tired. I know there are very few people, if any, who truly understand what you do every day. I am sure there are times you have questioned your decision to become a teacher, but I want to remind you that you have the power to change lives. Don't give up!

Sincerely,

A High School Dropout

Dr. Dayna Smith,
Director of Special Programs
Orangefield, Texas

You Are a Capeless Hero   13

Dear Teacher,

As you sit here reading this letter, you are probably surrounded by stacks of ungraded and graded papers feeling defeated or possibly relieved that you are actually sitting. You have been giving of yourself to so many people today, and there's a slight possibility that no one poured into you today.

As a principal and former teacher, I want you to know that you are appreciated in this very moment no matter what you are currently doing. You have done the work! You have taken constructive criticism! You have embodied the task of wearing multiple hats! Your efforts are not going unnoticed no matter how you may feel.

I would like you to get up and look into a mirror or put your phone's camera in selfie mood. The image/reflection that you see is that of a capeless hero. You're not forgotten. There's a child sitting at home thinking of your kind words. There's a struggling child staying up late to study, because you believed in them. There's a parent that's searching for resources, because you equipped them with the tools they needed to help their child. There's a child "playing school" in their bedroom, because you planted a seed.

You are making impactful waves in this world, and you're doing it solely by being a dedicated educator. Is it always easy? No. Is it always fun? No, but it's definitely worth it.

You put your soul into this job, and it shows. Guess what? If you missed it at work today, there's always tomorrow. That's the beauty of waking up each day. You have the chance to be great on purpose. That kid needs you! The teacher next door needs you. Your presence is worth more than you'll ever know. Some people tend to show admiration by not acknowledging you or your efforts. Look around you! They're emulating your ideas. Don't get caught up in the applause, because it is often silent.

DOI: 10.4324/9781003216988-13

Keep doing what you're doing, but get better at it each day! If no one else tells you, Dr. George loves you.

Dr. Belinda George
Principal
Beaumont, TX

You Are Valuable.
Complete. Loved.

Dear Teacher,

Where do I begin?

I have so many things I should so admire and appreciate about you.

I wanted to take this time to pause, reflect and communicate to you what a powerful impact you've made and continue to make on so many lives that cross your path.

So often in the emptiness of our classrooms, during the early morning or late evening hours of what seems like endless grading…

I know we often ask, "am I making a difference? does anybody really care? would it even matter if I wasn't here tomorrow?"

The answer dear teacher… is yes, yes and yes!

You, my dear teacher, are so Valuable. So Complete. So Loved!

Do you not know you have instilled a legacy deep down inside the students you have taught that will last generations! You are a lifesaver… a game changer!

I love the way that you are such a powerful role model and care about your students long after they graduated.

I love how you care about not only their current success but their success in the future even beyond academics.

I love how you have such a way about you that creates an environment inside your classroom for every student to feel they belong, are safe and smart.

I love how you love even the unlovable and would do anything for them.

And I love how you accept nothing but their very best and push them to reach for their full potential.

Your endless passion to reach students is contagious throughout the campus. You are truly the teacher the students

DOI: 10.4324/9781003216988-14

will line up outside your door waiting to get in, just to be known as one of "your" precious students.

"Thank you" just doesn't touch the surface of the gratitude I have for you. I want you to know… I am a better person, colleague, teacher, educator because of you.

I am eternally grateful!

It's a great day to be alive!

Dr. Jeff Springer
Educational Coach, Consultant
Magnolia, Texas

Being Comfortable with Uncomfortable

15

Dear Teacher,

UNCOMFORTABLE. What emotion do you feel when you see this word? Eight years ago when I was a teacher, I felt a negative emotion when situations made me uncomfortable. Fast forward to now as a school counselor and that word means something else to me. I will always be a teacher at heart because that is how my journey began. In the beginning of my career I was always hungry for more. I was a physical education teacher and athletic coach so you can imagine the busy schedule. Negative and uncomfortable situations would arise and I would just sit there in it. I would never find a way out; I also would not grow in it as well.

I want to backtrack some and tell you how this journey started so that you may see why I ended up the way I did. My mother passed away in 2006 from ovarian cancer and that forever changed my life. I was lucky enough that she was able to see me walk to obtain my diploma but she never was able to see me gain my first job as an educator. I wanted to make her proud and that was my push to start searching for jobs.

I will always be grateful for the eight years I was in Beaumont ISD at Odom Academy. This job shaped me and was instrumental in my journey as an educator. Til this day I am still close friends with the educators I worked with and also some of my students. As a coach, I had most of my athletes come to me for guidance and assistance with personal or academic issues. I knew then that my journey was about to take a turn. I have been a school counselor for almost six years and I truly know this is my calling.

After Covid happened my career took a different direction and just ran with it. One of the biggest reasons I took those risks was because I surrendered to those uncomfortable situations and I searched for how they could help me grow. And let me tell you!! The growth has not stopped! I urge you to seek out those uncomfortable situations. If I am not uncomfortable, then I am not growing. I also urge you to seek out opportunities to learn and grow because those two things should never stop!

You were meant to be in this career, and for some this career chose you. I won't lie and say that the stress will not be there and on some days you might feel like breaking. But the joys, the happy tears, the laughs, the connections, the growth, the learning, and the changes you will make with your students will always outweigh the bad. Be the change agent with the servant heart!

Sincerely,

Dyann Wilson
@tms_counselor
#techCAREtwins

Exactly You

16

Dear Teacher,

Question – Do you feel worthy? I know sometimes I don't. Worthiness in education is tough. We're constantly being bombarded by Facebook groups, Pinterest posts and TikTok teachers. And, I don't know about you, but I work with some *incredible* educators, who I am continuously comparing myself to. All this to say, if you find yourself feeling unworthy, you're not alone! But I'm here to let you in on a secret... You are EXACTLY who you need to be for the kids in YOUR classroom.

I want you to think about your students for a second. Are they all exactly the same? Heck no! And that's precisely what makes them great! We teach our kids all the time that our differences are what set us apart. SPOILER ALERT!!! The same thing goes for teachers! If we were all exactly the same, we would literally be doing an injustice to our students. We all bring something different to the table and by working collaboratively, we are able to meet our students' diverse and unique needs.

Did you know that we all have something, as an educator, that we're experts at? You might not have really thought about it, because in education we're trained to look at our areas for growth, NOT our areas of expertise. But it's true! So the next time you're comparing yourself to your fellow teachers, think about something that YOU do that's amazing and ask yourself, how does this skill benefit my students? I bet you'll be surprised to realize that you're making a tremendous impact on each of their lives.

I'll leave you with this – I believe in YOU! I believe that you are doing AMAZING things. I believe that your classroom is full

DOI: 10.4324/9781003216988-16

of love, of laughter and of learning. Thank you for everything that you do. You are WORTHY! Don't forget it.

Elena Ortiz
Kindergarten Teacher
Prosper, Texas

Carpe Diem! The Best Views Always Come from the Toughest People and Hardest Climbs

17

Dear Teacher,

Someone once said, "The best view comes after the hardest climb," so my question to you is… how's the view? 2020–2021 has undoubtedly been the "mountain" of all mountains when it comes to "the climb." Since March of 2020, our world especially as an educator has been rocked, and forever changed with the ripple effects of the pandemic and school as we once knew it. Summer break has finally created the moment where we can catch our breath, as we somehow made it through this unthinkable academic year of learning.

As a proud high school principal, I had a front row seat to the miracles that you all have courageously made happen over the past year. In March of 2020 you went from face-to-face school to completely virtual school in under a couple of weeks as this global pandemic really forced the entire world to shut down. People lost jobs, homes, loved ones, friends… and essentially part of their joy and hope. With virtually no warning or training you still climbed… and made it happen. Your unwavering commitment, resiliency, passion, grace, and grit were all used to do what you could to help our students while juggling your own family's needs at the same time. This was living proof that toughness is part of one's soul and spirit, not strictly muscles. The Senior Class of 2020 was missing out on so much, but I saw

DOI: 10.4324/9781003216988-17

you never settle and do everything in your power to ensure they were still celebrated and applauded; even if some parts had to be virtual, we still pulled off a graduation ceremony that brought closure and recognition to these deserving young adults. That was huge!

When the summer of 2020 came, we all had a hope that with the six-month global shutdown we would finally be able to experience a normal start in the new school year by Fall. But as the pandemic quickly taught us, the "uncontrollables" were still there as COVID continued to throw avalanches our way… there was no vaccine available to us yet, safety protocols were a mile long, we had to enforce everyone was wearing masks, sanitizing, and social distancing by at least six feet in an over-crowded building. Yet, the biggest obstacle was that families were given the choice to choose virtual learning or face-to-face learning for their student based on their own health and safety needs, so I watched you set your own well-being aside and pour 150 percent each day into your lessons, teaching virtually and face to face in the same period and constantly trying to reach each and every child with courses of 150–175 students.

What I was blessed to witness was nothing short of a miracle. I witnessed your tears as you tirelessly worked for hours, including most weekends, to lesson plan, make videos, and host tutorials before school, after school, and even during your lunch time to do your absolute best to reach and teach your students. I witnessed bravery to try new things, things that even failed a few times, but more importantly I witnessed you bounce back even stronger and better that even you thought you could. I witnessed that you were there for way more than academics; you were the social and emotional support lifeline for many of our students' mental health breakdowns that we have seen throughout this pandemic. I witnessed you dig deep, through pure mental and physical exhaustion, and even some public scrutiny to continue showing up and climbing each and every day until the end of the school year, because you chose kids over your own welfare most days. (Side note – check out what Brené Brown says about the people not in the arena with you… truth!) I saw how the little appreciation things like ice cream bars, lemonade stands, and kindness cards produced happy tears and glimpses of "ok, I will give it one more try," as I tried my best as your leader to support and celebrate you so that we could dig deep to just keep climbing.

Yes, this year… I witnessed miracles performed by the most dedicated, hardworking, innovative, and persistent group of people I have ever known… teachers! Here are my takeaways: 1. The climb will always be easier if you find the right group (your tribe) of people to go with you! 2. If you find something that works… share… we are all on the same climbing journey together for student emotional and academic success! 3. Appreciation is the real motivator; don't forget to pay it forward to others, because it never goes unnoticed or felt and positive ripple effects are contagious. Teachers, you are loved, you are valued, and you are the bright light in our young people's lives… so rest up… and never quit being you, because the best views will always come from the toughest people and hardest climbs! Carpe diem and much love!

Heather Patterson
Principal, George Ranch High School
Richmond, Texas

Hear Me, See Me, Know Me

18

Dear Teacher,

If you really knew me, you would know the answers to the questions you so frequently ask.

Why don't I show you respect? If you really knew me, you would know that I don't know you. How can I trust and respect someone when I haven't gotten the same in return? Not from so-called friends; not from family; not from teachers. I don't even know what respect looks like.

Why don't I answer when you call on me? If you really knew me, you would know I am scared to death to be humiliated when I answer incorrectly. It's just easier to put my head down.

Why do I laugh at inappropriate times or have anger outbursts in the middle of class? If you really knew me, you would know that if I showed my real emotions, I would just cry.

Why didn't I complete my homework? If you really knew me, you would know that after my mom died and my dad started working two jobs, I've had to take care of my younger siblings and my homework has to take a backseat.

Why am I not responding to your encouragement? If you really knew me, you would know I am confused. I've always been told I won't amount to anything so what is it that *you* see? Your expectations are too high and you will just be disappointed.

Why am I not grateful that you are saying nice things to me? If you really knew me, you would know that it makes me uncomfortable because no one has ever talked that way to me. Or when they have, they wanted something from me that should be too precious to give away.

These are just some of the questions I've heard teachers ask and the answers I've heard students say over my 28-year career

DOI: 10.4324/9781003216988-18

as a counselor and social worker in the schools. I could fill pages and pages of heart-wrenching situations I've encountered. No doubt, you have all been taught what students need to succeed. They need consistency, structure, predictability, unconditional love, intentional kindness, empathy, understanding, stability, persistence, humor, honesty, positivity and compassion, just to name a few. I would like to expand on a few key points I have learned over the years.

My greatest advice to you is to Listen. Really listen. I think we as educators feel we have it all figured out. We predict behavior and assume we know the reason behind the behavior. We think back to a former student who acted "just like that" so this kid should have the same explanation, right? Other times we see ourselves in some of these students so we think we know exactly what will work with that child: what worked with you. In our heads we think: "That happened to me, so I know exactly how they are feeling." Then we change our focus and try to "fix" them. We try to teach them what they should and shouldn't do and how they should feel. Rarely does it work out that way.

Why are we still struggling to connect with that child? Why aren't your proven interventions working? We get confused because we are so kind to all students. We treat every kid equally because we know the importance of being fair. That, in and of itself, is part of the problem. We need to shift our focus to Equity. Dr. Pedro Noguera states it best: "Equality is giving everyone shoes. Equity is giving everyone shoes that fit." Find each child's interests, talents, challenges, and uniqueness.

Stop trying to define them by their behavior or their circumstances. The behavior they are exhibiting right now does not define WHO they are or who they are going to become. It may explain a few things, but that's just a minor piece in the puzzle. They are so much more. If you really want to make an impact, listen to them and let it resonate in your heart. Find the potential in every child. We can't demand students to strive for their full potential when we can't even see it ourselves. I know, sometimes it seems you are constantly digging to find that one thing to help them dream. It's hard work. Persevere, because when you find it, incredible things will happen! Not only will their lives change forever, so will yours.

Side note: Kids see through fake. "Fake it till you make it" is not going to work with kids. It may get you through some of your own personal issues, but it will not work with these students. They have X-ray vision when it comes to genuineness. Don't force yourself to like a child. Just do it—really find something—ANYTHING—grab onto it and truly like that child. Encourage them. Understand them. Acknowledge them.

I have been facilitating grief groups at the middle school and high school levels for over 20 years. The one thing that is constant every single year: no one person's grief journey is the same. There may be similarities: they may have both lost a parent; they may have lost a loved one to an illness, an accident, or suicide; they may have lost the exact same person. But I guarantee their experience, their behavior, their feelings, their perspectives are not the same. Their journey will not be the same.

Isn't life just a journey, too? It is filled with joys, sorrows, obstacles, challenges, successes, failures. Every single person has a story. Some will tell their stories, some will not. It's still *their* story and *their* journey. It's not our purpose as educators to get all the details of the story, nor is it our mission to make sure they share that story. It IS our purpose and mission to be by their side as they navigate through their journey. Listen. Really listen. Compassionately, intentionally, and genuinely. If you do that, they will no longer think, "if you really knew me". Because you will.

Jaime Cunningham
Youth Service Specialist
San Leon, Texas

The Walker, the Talker, and You

19

Dear Teacher,

You are making a difference. Trust me, I know that some days it just doesn't seem that way. But you are.

You know the student who comes into your room a few extra times a week just to say hello? He needs you. You know the student who doesn't seem to smile much but you feel it a personal victory when she does? She needs you. You know that student who comes to visit you just to say hello? He needs you. You are making a difference. The talker. The walker. The joker. THE TALKER. The one who needs you the most and you don't even know it. You are making an indelible mark on each student you have in your room, whether that student meets you with a friend passing through or is a student you teach for days, weeks or years.

I truly believe that teaching chooses us; we don't choose teaching. We think we do. You were born to be a teacher. Each and every turn and twist in your path led you right where you belong. Here. Today. Reading this book and connecting with other teachers because there is power in numbers.

Hold your head high, even when the weight of the world is on your shoulders. You have the power to change lives. You are changing lives.

Hugs,

Jen Henson
Founder: Jen Henson ACT Prep
Montgomery, Texas

DOI: 10.4324/9781003216988-19

It's Not About You

20

Dear Teacher,

It's not about you!

You may believe you can't take it when a kid with extreme behavior kicks you, hits you, and cusses the most unbelievable profanity at you. **It's not about you** – the kid is communicating with you the only way they know best. All behavior is communication, and we just have to learn and understand this language.

You may take a kid's behavior personally, and ask, "How can they treat us like this?" **It's not about you** – taking a kid's behavior personally sets us up for not being able to understand them. We are selfish to think that this behavior is because of our actions. Again, a kid is communicating with us the best way they know how.

You may state out loud to kids, parents, or colleagues, "You can't do that in my classroom. This behavior is unacceptable." **It's not about you** – first, it is our classroom. All kids play a role in building the culture of the classroom. Get over the fact that the classroom is yours… it's "ours!" Second, we need to understand the behavior, the trigger, and understand if the kid possesses the tools and strategies to change their behavior. With dysregulation, we must first co-regulate with the kid before they can regulate on their own behavior. We can't start this process if the classroom is "mine" and you believe "I don't allow this behavior."

You may believe a parent should be addressing this behavior at home so we can finally teach. We even tell a parent, "If only you would take care of this outburst at home, I can do my job." **It's not about you** – parents are doing the best they can with the tools and strategies they possess. This is their current reality. We need to take kids where they are, as well as parents, and set goals as a team. This may include putting new tools and strategies into both students' and parents' toolboxes.

DOI: 10.4324/9781003216988-20

You may think I am not caring teacher. **It's not about you** – if you chose teaching you must be that consistent, caring teacher that connects with students, and continues to connect with students that treat us the worst. Kids with extreme behaviors search out predictability. If they can predict how you are going to react, over time their behavior will change as long as you are exhibiting kindness, caring, and calmness. These traits are contagious. We can then start to predict their behaviors.

You may think the kid hates you. **It's not about you** – please understand that when a kid truly cares for you, they take out their emotions with extreme behaviors on those that care about them the most and that are safe. This phenomenon is hard to understand as a teacher. When we think this kid may hate us, they may be actually testing us. They are testing us to see how we are going to react. Error on the side of compassion, which is empathy in action…so, take action!

You may believe the classroom would be safer without this kid. **It's not about you** – provide that learning environment that is safe, because we may not know how safe a student's home may be. What kids are going home to over summer break, Christmas break, every Friday, and possibly every night, may not be safe. Chaos may be all around them, so make the classroom and school a safe place, always!

You may think, "I can't work with this kid, I am giving up." **It's not about you** – don't give up on a child even if it feels like nothing is working. Many kids are used to their caregivers giving up them. They know that if they show these extreme behaviors everyone gets mad, yells or hits them, or leaves them, which becomes predictable to them. Be predictable, never give up on a kid.

You may believe you don't have the time to understand a student's outbursts. **It's not about you** – dig deeper into the behavior, find the trigger, work with your team at school to wrap around all services for this kid. So many times we give consequences for a behavior when we do not even know what the trigger was, why the behavior is occurring, and what the kid's life looked and sounded like from after school the previous day until they came into the classroom today. Take the time to dig deeper to understand; you may be the only one that does!

You may believe you can't stick up for a kid that acts this way. **It's not about you** – all kids need that one person who was an advocate for them no matter what. Treat every student like they are your own. Under the same premise as you are your own child's best advocate (hopefully), be that advocate for the tough kid. That kid may not have anyone else.

You may believe you are not making a difference in a child's life. **It's not about you** – understand that students will remember more about how you treated them than the content you teach. As adults we remember back to our most influential teachers in our lives. It was not that they taught us about the separation of powers in government class, it was the fact that they cared about us. It shows with their words and actions. Think to yourself, how do you want to be remembered by your students?

Since it isn't about you, make a difference every day with your students!

With Greatest Love for the Tough Kids,

Jon Konen
Superintendent
Corvallis, Montana

Nine Roles

21

Dear Teacher,

As an educator, I have discovered that when I share my profession with others, I often will hear negative comments, mostly others apologizing and confirming how sorry they feel for me. I have never understood these apologies, because as educators, we truly have one of the most important roles on earth.

Our jobs are numerous. When I began teaching years ago, I literally believed my job would simply be to show up, be prepared and teach. This could not be further from the truth. Our role is as mom or dad to kids in need. We play nurse to those who don't feel well. We are professional huggers when students need love. We are crisis counselors for those kids whose world just crashed around them. And more than likely, we perform all these roles before 9:30AM. We are so much more than content and curriculum. We are mentors leading students to an incredible future. We are motivational speakers to kids who want to find their passion. We are hearts, and minds, and souls, and creativity and relationships.

There will be days when you will feel defeated, challenged, drained, and alone. There will be mornings when four cups of coffee just won't cut it. There will be nights when you leave a red wine stain on the 100 papers you grade until midnight. There will be that ONE student that will make you reassess your entire career choices. This will also be the one student who is never absent. There will always be a parent that is smarter than you and will tell you how to do your job. But always remember this… Your passion and your energy and your joy will pass directly to your students. They will benefit from your smiles every single day. For some of your students, you will be the most important person in their life. You will be the one educator they will fondly remember when they begin their own futures. To some kids, you will be the only one who makes them feel safe.

DOI: 10.4324/9781003216988-21

We are the biggest influencers to these kids! Inspire them every day. Allow them freedom to think and to share. Listen when they talk to you. Build relationships with them. Your passion WILL spread within the classroom. And when you bring passion into the classroom, you will love everything about teaching.

So, blast the music every day. Wear a tutu once a week. Stand on the desks during instruction. Toss glitter everywhere for no reason at all. Speak all day with a British accent. Take your classroom outside. Jump on the chairs and sing.

Dress up.
Show up.
But never ever give up!
You rock. You matter. You are awesome. You can do this. Be the Bad-Ass of the Class.

Fondly,

Jonna Patterson
6th Grade Teacher
Richmond, Texas

All Gas, No Brakes! **22**

Dear Teacher,

Congratulations! You have chosen to be a part of the greatest profession this side of the pearly gates. What an opportunity you have each day to have an influence on the youth of our world. That influence can be positive or negative. The great thing is that you get to choose which one it will be. It is my hope in writing you this letter that I can help you find ways to make the influence you have on your students the most rewarding and positive experience of their lives and yours as well.

I am entering year 23 as an educator and between my schooling starting at age five, college, and then starting my career, education has been a part of my life for the past 40 years. As you can tell, I have a passion and a belief in the importance of the roles teachers have in the world. I want to share some things that have helped me keep my focus on the power of my influence over my career so far.

1. **The students are NOT coming to school to serve my needs; it is my job to serve them and their needs.**
   I am not sure I have always seen it this way, but as I have gained experience I know that when my work day is over if I have served my students I go home with a feeling of joy and accomplishment. Serving can be different things for different people and it can be different from day to day. It may be an ear to listen, advice to give, encouragement through a tough time, modeling behavior or just words that let them know you love them and care about them. We may be the only adult they have in their lives to show them the right way to do things. At the end of the day, it's amazing how serving others can make my day so much better. So, wake up each day searching for a way to serve your students and your days will be blessed.

DOI: 10.4324/9781003216988-22

Just like with students, you are who you hang around.
A school can mirror society in a lot of ways. One of those ways is you tend to become like the people you hang around. I tell my students that all the time. Those you choose to be around will have an influence on how you think and act. Even if you are the one exception to that rule, you will still be lumped in with that group with how they act and behave. I bring that up because where you hang out and who you hang around at school can influence you and your attitude. If you hang around negative people that complain all the time guess what you will be doing before too long. I don't know about you but the days when I spend most of my time being negative and complaining about things, I have never gone home in a good mood, sat down on the couch and said, "Man what a great day today!" Most likely the next words to come out of my mouth are "I can't believe I have to go back there tomorrow." When I am around co-workers that are positive it is amazing how much better my day goes. It is amazing how much better I feel when I get home and how much more excited I am to go back to go work the next day. You want to get more joy from a day of work and a better appreciation of what you do: don't hang around complainers and negative people. Find the positive, uplifters, life speaking people and go join their group. You will see the difference.

3. **Gas up the tank.**
There is so much negativity today, you have to find a way to "gas up the tank." What I mean by that is you have to find a way to put positive thoughts, ideas, memories etc. into your mind and body on a continuous basis. Like putting gas into a gas tank, there has to be some fuel in the body to keep you going. One thing that I do is read a book or two each summer that keep me focused on becoming a better person and teacher. Books about successful people or businesses can give me some kind of insight as to how to improve myself and my approach to my job. Sometimes it may just be one thing that sticks

out, but that one thing can be the spark that sets the forest on fire.

Another thing I do is re-read letters from past students, parents, or co-workers. I do not keep these things and read them to make myself feel good or as a symbol of how great I am. I keep them and re-read them to remind myself of the reasons why I do what I do for a living. Those letters that say "thanks", "I love you coach", or "thank you for everything you have done for my son" remind me that at some point in my career, no matter the mistakes I have made, I did something good enough for a student or parent to take time to sit down and write a letter of thanks. That's a great feeling. Take some time to reflect on those things. It is not boasting or bragging, it is simply a reminder that if you made that kind of an impact on someone's life once, you can do it again. There is no better fuel than that.

I hope this helps you in your journey as an educator. No matter what, LOVE your students. Give them your best. Be a blessing to them and the profession. There is no better profession on earth.

Your brother in the service

Josh Smalley
Athletic Director/Head Football Coach
Orangefield, TX | Orangefield ISD

Be Enough

23

Dear Teacher,

You have embarked on a weathering journey that is unpredictable, to say the least, and requires many changes and the utmost flexibility of you. Some days will be harder than others; some seemingly impossible. Whatever you do, whatever is said, no matter how you feel, in any circumstance and every situation, remember…

You Are Enough.

As a teacher, I decided long ago that I would love each and every one of my students, as if they were my own. This is the hardest route to take, but the most fulfilling journey. Making your love, passion and commitment to your students personal gives you a fresh outlook on the hope, encouragement, pedagogy and life-preparation you give. It is never going to be perfect; for you will never be perfect. Show students that perfection does not breed success. Admit your faults, apologize when needed, and always begin, continue and finish again.

You Are Enough.

When the weather of life is bad, and you're buried in the chaotic tornado of lesson plans, grading, projects and parents, find shelter in the presence of positive colleagues. They can help you stand against the blustering winds and the heavy downpours that are inevitable. You may be battered and bruised, but you can stand, in the rubble and dismay, still thriving and working for your students. Do not run and hide and leave someone else to clean up the mess. You can do this.

You Are Enough.

DOI: 10.4324/9781003216988-23

This profession will make you beam with pride at something you have worked hours on preparing. You have dotted every I, crossed every T. This will be the perfect lesson for your students! They are going to love it! You anticipate the moment you get to share all of your hard work with them... and it fails. You fall flat. It bombs. Crickets... Nothing would feel better, at that moment, than if the earth would quake, open up and swallow you. Then you don't have to burn under their disappointing glare and the wonder of what comes next. Take a breath. Steady yourself in the frame of all you have learned and go again. Always remember that you can redo, retell and reteach. Show your students that sometimes you have to try twice to reach your goal.

You Are Enough.

Students come to us seeking: knowledge, power, acceptance, reassurance, the simplest of love. You have the power to extend all of these to them. In the midst of your doubt, and the tsunami of tears that often comes, from you and the students, remember that you have to see clearly to find your way. Wipe away the tears and search for what each student needs. Some just need to be seen. Others need tangible help. Give of your heart, freely. Beware; this does mean that your heart will be broken, trampled and crushed, at some point. You are strong enough, smart enough, resilient enough, loving enough and giving enough.

You Are Enough.

I believe you are placed in the classroom, in the hall, at the school, in the district where you are meant to be. You are there to change the life of one, or many. No matter the trials, no matter the pain, no matter the hurt, you are there because you are meant to be. You are the light that will shine in the darkest night, you are the shelter that some student will seek, you are the compass to lead them out of the wilderness, you are the lifeline they crave...

You Are Enough.

Never let all that flies at you dictate all that you will do. Keep the energy, nurturing, optimism, understanding, grace and humility your students need to see.

Be Enough.

Kecia Wade Dennis
Teacher/Coach
Richland Hills, Texas

You, Yes You

24

Dear Teacher,

If no one ever says thank you for ALL you do, let me say it… thank you. Thank you for being one of God's greatest gifts on earth. You are needed, you are loved, you are appreciated, and you are unforgettable.

Please don't give up when you can't keep up with all the paperwork. Please don't give up when your students seem like they don't want to listen or learn. Please don't give up when you have more kids in your classroom than you have room for. Please don't give up when you don't have all the resources you need because of lack of funding. Please don't give up when you don't get to go to the bathroom when you need to go. Please don't give up when you don't have time to eat the lunch you prepared because you have to make a few more copies or call a student's parent. Please don't give up when parents are complaining about you to others. Please don't give up when you seem to do more than everyone else. Please don't give up when that one student just can't seem to get it right and you've tried everything. Please don't give up when you're too tired and don't feel like you have anything else to give. You are needed, dear teacher.

You may not receive an award or get a gift for teacher appreciation week. You may even have a student who is defiant and refuses to take direction from you, let alone instruction. You may have a student who curses you every day or turns over desks and chairs like it's their job to but let me say thank you. You are loved, dear teacher.

For the numerous things you do for students that no one knows about, for all the money you spend that you'll never be reimbursed for, for the enthusiastic and engaging lessons that make your classroom the most fun place on earth, and for all the tears you've cried due to stress, let me say thank you. You are appreciated, dear teacher.

DOI: 10.4324/9781003216988-24

So many children need your love, your time, your creativity, your hugs, your high-fives, your good morning greetings, your goodbye sendoffs, your I love you, your encouragement, your advice, your redirection, your wisdom, your smile, your creativity, and your heart. Not everyone can do that and that is what makes you so necessary. No pay scale can match the countless papers you grade, the immeasurable amount of parent contacts you make, the hours of planning you do in school and at home, the numerous complaints you get from parents and students or the well-deserved thank you that you may never receive but let me say thank you. You are unforgettable, dear teacher.

Ms. Keevie Vincent
Elementary Teacher
Henderson, KY.

Seen

25

Dear Teacher,

I see you…

- I see you doing double, triple the work that you've done in years past.
- I see you skipping lunch to run copies, talk to that student, run to the bathroom, make that quick phone call, take care of that personal matter that you won't have time to do after school.
- I see you doing tutoring with that student in your classroom after hours in the hopes that a just a little bit more of you will make the difference.
- I see you staying late getting things done in preparation for tomorrow.
- I see you coming in early.
- I see the fortifying sip of coffee, tea, soda before the kids coming in and your smile and natural energy take over.
- I see you coming up with amazing lessons in the car, in the shower, in the bed at night when you can't sleep.
- I see the hours on Pinterest, Teachers Pay Teachers and Google trying to plan and research to make learning relevant and fresh and interesting.
- I see the money you spend from your own pocket, taken from your own families, from your own life to buy pencils, pens, decorations, glue, things for the classroom.
- I see the fire in your heart for YOUR kids; these students who will always be in your heart even when they are no longer in your grade.
- I see the love and devotion to your craft to be better for them, to do more for them, to love them where they lack.
- I see you supporting your kiddos, going to their games, events, performances so they'll know even if their parents

DOI: 10.4324/9781003216988-25

don't go, there will be at least one loving face in the crowd just for them.

I see you trying to reach that one bubble kid...the kid who with just a little bit more love, patience, attention is going to be amazing. You know it.

I know how you're not supposed to play favorites, but I see how that one special student worms their way into your heart more than the others.

I see the way you reach out to your students, the way you build connection and relationship, so that you're not just a teacher, you're *their* teacher.

I see you.

I see you standing at the front of the room doing your all to keep their attention. If they'd just pay attention, this lesson would be awesome.

I see you making parent contact even though you've called countless times before and nothing has been done.

I see you with that side hustle, trying to make ends meet.

I see you taking things home and then feeling guilty because they never came out of your bag.

I see you spending hours away from family and friends doing work that "has to be done" for Monday.

I see your frustration as more and more gets piled on, almost daily it sometimes seems, things that admin says won't be hard, that will just take a second to implement.

I see how they don't have a clue.

I see your exhaustion at the end of the day, the result from being "on" all day.

I see you rushing to get your grades, lesson plans, attendance done.

I see you making it by the hair of your teeth.

I see the guilt from feeling like you're not doing your all any-where... not at home, not at work.

I see you.

I see you getting to school later and later each day as the year wears on.

I see you binging Netflix on the weekend, thinking about the grading you should do, the lesson planning that needs to be done, but I see your lack of motivation, too.

I see you on the weekend too tired to do anything, too overwhelmed, too paralyzed by your to-do list, and so you do… nothing.

I see you thinking "just one more episode" and I see that single episode that turns into three that turns into four that turns into the entire season.

I see you sitting at your desk feeling like a failure, as the work stacks up.

I see how their poor planning constitutes your emergency, and that puts you even further behind.

I see you promising yourself to do better, to be better next time.

I see how this year wears on you.

I see how you covertly research online other ways to make money with your degree.

I see you looking at pay scales for other districts, how you put out feelers wondering if that administration treats their teachers better than yours does.

I see how you feel like a failure because you're slacking in areas where you never have before.

I see how you are May-tired long before it's May.

I see how weary you are, how done you are with it all.

I see you.

I'm not going to participate in toxic positivity and tell you to do it for the outcome and not the income.

I'm not going to say it will get better.

I'm not going to lie to you with platitudes.

I'm simply going to say I see you.

I see all you do.

I know you are tired.

What you do is enough.
YOU are enough.

I see you.

I am you.

We are enough, dear teacher.
Take care of you.
Love,

Kris Bowers
High School English
Princeton, Texas

A Veteran Teacher's Advice for the Tough Days

26

Dear Teacher,

Teaching is the best job ever in so many ways, and it is also the most challenging. Some days, we just need a little bit of encouragement, and these are the words I wish someone would have told me when I needed to hear them.

#1) Be true to yourself.

There is only ONE of you in the entire universe, and you have your own creative set of skills and quirks that makes you an amazing person and teacher. Keep that! Bring it every day to your classroom. Embrace it. And don't spend one second thinking about "what will they think if I do…"

One of my favorite people in education is Dave Burgess because his book introduced me to the idea of "Teach Like a Pirate!" and all I had heard up until that point was that I was going to forever be the "weirdo" who just never quite fit in within the education world. After learning about the "Teach Like a Pirate" philosophy, I embraced my own nerdiness… showing kids my "gamer" and anime nerd self, and they loved it. It helped me connect with students on a whole different level; and it also helped them embrace their own unique qualities. We learned to be a better community, instead of just all trying to fit into a "type-A" robot, everything has to be perfect mentality. Other teachers on campus started to notice a change in my teaching as

DOI: 10.4324/9781003216988-26

well. Now, talking with other veteran teachers on campus, they always say "you've really come a long way as a teacher… and it shows! You're great for the kids!"

What do I think made the difference? I stopped caring what other people thought about the way I taught in my classroom, and I just started being myself and true to my own philosophy of education. I could not be happier!

#2) Have a growth mindset.

It's so easy to take everything personally when administrators or instructional coaches come and offer feedback. It's even more frustrating when a growth plan is suggested. But here's the thing. If someone is taking time to offer you feedback, at least on some level, it means that they care, and they are invested in making you better. Does that mean that you should DO everything they say? Not necessarily… go back and see my first piece of advice. But DO take what they say to heart. Where are they coming from? What do they see that you don't? Is there a way that you can incorporate what they suggest while still doing what you believe is best for your students in your classroom? If so, then what does it hurt to try something they suggest?

I remember being so hurt and frustrated (and angry, if I'm being honest) the year my administrator decided to put me on a growth plan. I thought it was stupid when I saw that my growth plan wasn't even about how I taught, but rather my lack of communication with other adults in my profession. I didn't see the value or the purpose. Looking back, however, I realize that the year I was on a growth plan was actually a year that my teaching life changed significantly. I was forced out of my comfort zone, and I was challenged to look at new ways of thinking and interacting with other educators.

As I look back to where I was THEN (several years ago) to where I am NOW, I am GRATEFUL for that "awful" growth plan because without it, I doubt I would have challenged myself to begin reaching toward my own educational goals (like becoming a national presenter to teachers!). I look over my experiences getting to be interviewed by great educators like Hal Bowman and Todd Nesloney. Before that growth plan which FORCED me to stop being an introverted teacher, I would have NEVER dreamed of reaching out to either of them, never asking questions about "how do you...". Now, I'm going into my 14th year in education, taking steps toward my goal of being an educator who can bring out the greatness in students and other teachers by sharing my passion of teaching.

When others offer you advice or suggestions on your classroom and work, LISTEN. Think about it. Take what they say and MAKE IT YOUR OWN. You can implement things that they suggest while still remaining true to what you believe to be best practice in your classroom.

And, on the contrary, if it's just NOT going to work, be WILLING to have that conversation with them. Advice and suggestions are that... a starting point for a CONVERSATION. Education is about working together to help the students reach their fullest potential both inside and outside a classroom, and it takes all of us to do that! So have a conversation!

#3) (this is MOST important) NEVER FORGET YOUR WHY.

One thing that breaks my teacher heart is when my colleagues get burnt out and want to (or do) leave teaching. Or they refuse to connect with other educators in social media because all they hear about is the negativity. I hate when our conversations become focused on the bad things. When this happens, go back to your why. Remember it. Think about it, and then ask yourself if you are living up to your "why."

Sometimes, we get stuck in the negative, and sometimes it IS hard to get back to the positive, but remembering your why is a great first step. I am reminded of my why any time I remember my students who struggled the most experiencing their first feelings of success after swearing "You can try everything you want, but we'll NEVER be good at this..." Their faces, their smiles, their success... MY WHY. What's yours? What makes you wake up every day ready to teach? Always remember that. It makes a difference!

Sincerely,

Kristi M. Everhart
Dyslexia/Reading Intervention
Lockhart Junior High
Lockhart, Texas

Unconditional Compassion

27

Dear Teacher,

I would like for you to bring to mind your students.

Call to mind the students that are hard-working and push themselves beyond what they think they are capable of. Their tenacity is fueled by your praise and encouragement. They achieve because of your unwavering belief that they can. You inspire them to celebrate and savor every success, no matter how large or how small.

Next, bring to mind your students who have struggled and get discouraged by their challenges. Whether their difficulties resulted from external or internal circumstances, what were the words of kindness and support that you offered them? Letting them know you were behind them one hundred percent, *especially when they felt defeated*, allows them to trust in your unconditional care and keeps them going.

Lastly, think of your students that are hard to reach. They may have made poor choices and mistakes, but you aren't going to give up on them. Even when it seems like there is no way to get through, you offer them a compassion and acceptance that they may not feel for themselves.

As a teacher, you know more than anyone that words of encouragement feed the fire of resilience far more than words of judgement. The compassion, kindness, and acceptance we have for our students is what inspires, encourages, and comforts them. It comes naturally to us and is a part of who we are.

But while it comes naturally to offer this warmth and support to our students, it comes less naturally to offer this same unconditional compassion, kindness, and acceptance to OURSELVES.

* * *

You, like many of your students, have most likely had many "wins" in recent weeks. These everyday achievements often don't

DOI: 10.4324/9781003216988-27

get the acknowledgement and celebration they deserve, but in the same way we encourage our students to celebrate and savor every success, we should offer ourselves the same experience.

You also most likely experienced many challenging moments these past several weeks. Sometimes the challenges are a result of external circumstances like class size, and other times the issues arise from internal circumstances like being too hard on ourselves. When we find ourselves in the midst of these struggles, we should offer ourselves the same words of kindness and support we offer to our students when they are struggling.

And just like the experiences of our most difficult students, sometimes it feels like we can't do anything right, and that the difficulties we have to deal with are insurmountable. It is when it seems like things are at their darkest that we need to offer ourselves even more warmth, compassion, and love.

* * *

When you bring to mind your students, the kindness and affection comes easily. When we think about offering these things to ourselves, we often hesitate and feel selfish or self-indulgent. We deny ourselves because we're not children or teens anymore, and we think that by now we should know better and be less forgiving.

But is that really true?

I would offer that it is not, and as such, my invitation to you is to expand the circle of your natural compassion, kindness, and acceptance so that it also includes yourself. Bask in it when things are going well, tap into it when facing challenges, and lean on it when you're at your lowest. You are as deserving of these sentiments as your students, and offering them to yourself will help ensure that you have the resilience to keep offering it to others for years to come.

Warmly,

Kristin McKeown
Teacher and Founder of TeachingBalance.com
Denver, Colorado

Authenticity Over Everything: Who We Are Matters

28

Dear Teacher,

You are enough,

Be yourself, everyone else is already taken.
Oscar Wilde

I want to thank you for being a part of the most important profession on the planet. I want to thank you for doing the work and changing the world. As a veteran teacher my biggest fear is that the knowledge and experiences of the previous generations will be lost by mine. I worry that the next generation of teachers will be less prepared for the classroom than we were. I take the responsibility of preparing the next generation of teachers seriously and hope this letter prevents you from making some of the mistakes that I did.

I used to think that content knowledge was the ticket to success as an educator. When I started teaching in 2009 the 2021 version of the internet was just being born. It was a time when the phrase *fake it till you make it* still applied. I thought I had to be the smartest person in the room. I thought I had to have all the answers. That is no longer the world we live in and to be honest it wasn't the world we lived in then. If I asked you to describe your favorite teacher you wouldn't talk about physics, grammar, or longitude and latitude. You would talk about a person and how they made you feel. You would describe their authenticity. You wouldn't wax poetic on the wonders of their content knowledge.

DOI: 10.4324/9781003216988-28

Dear Teacher – You are enough.

This profession can make you feel like you need to be someone else. That you need to fit into certain boxes in order to be a "great teacher." When my career started I was told to find a teacher who was having success, meaning good test scores, and copy what they were doing. As a new teacher I didn't know any better and spent the first couple of years of my career trying to be something that I was not. Regardless of what grade and content you teach there is one thing that all students want to learn – who you really are.

It does not matter what your personality is so long as your students see the real you. If you are an organized person then show your kids how to organize. If you are a dramatic theatre artist then be dramatic with your kids. If you are funny, be funny with your kids. Just don't be something you are not. Being real with your kids can be a scary proposition. Twitter, Instagram, and TikTok are filled with teachers who can make us feel like we are not enough. We see room transformations and classroom projects that we are not capable of creating. We measure our worth as educators against the highlight reels of others. By doing this we devalue ourselves and our gifts. You may also feel this on your campus. You may feel pressure to fit in. You may have people tell you to tone it down or turn it up. For the sake of our kids, please don't let your light be put into a box. Let your light shine to illuminate the path for others.

Dear Teacher – You are enough.

You may be worried about what students will think of the real you. Don't be. Our students see fake people all the time on TV and the internet. They are looking for people to show them what authenticity looks like. Our students may not know what authenticity is, but they sure know what it is not. We worry that if students see who we really are they won't like us. If we acknowledge the mistakes we've made to our students they won't respect us. We fear that if these two things are true then we will lose all credibility and we can't be an effective teacher. I have been through this and can promise you this isn't the case. The most important thing I have learned over the last decade in the classroom is this – our students are more forgiving than we ever imagine them to be. They are willing to forgive the mistakes of people who are genuine. They forgive the people that they trust.

Students are not required to build a relationship with us. They choose who they let into their world and it certainly won't be a teacher who is fake. Think back to how you would describe your favorite teacher. Now spin it forward to the end of your career. In thirty years what do you imagine your students saying about you? Does what they are saying in the future match what they see from you in the classroom today?

Our students live in a world in which they hear more and more that who they are is wrong. It seems that no matter who they see themselves as there is someone out there saying they are wrong. They feel like they shouldn't be who they actually are. This makes showing up in our authenticity so important for our kids. They don't need more people to tell them it is ok to be who they are. They need people to show them what it looks like to be who they really are. It isn't about them seeing themselves in you. It is about them seeing someone show up in their authenticity. Give your students permission to be who they are by being who you are.

P.S. If you ever need anything please reach out. We are family.

Much Love,

Kyle Krueger
Social Studies Teacher
The Twin Cities, Minnesota
@valueaddsvalue

Walking with a Passionate Purpose

29

Dear Teacher,

You are amazing! You are a talented and beautiful person! You are going to do great things in the lives of your students! Remind yourself of those things daily and speak them over yourself!

Despite what grade/age level you teach, curriculum that you use, or where you teach... the WHY or purpose of why we teach is all the same, and that is to make a difference in the lives of our students. Think about this... what other profession allows one to touch the lives of so many students or people in the span of one's career? When you stop and think about the impact that we have on the lives of our students that is an amazing thing. You may very well be the only smile and love that some of your students see or know, and that is an impact that will and can truly change lives. So, even on the hard days... and there will be hard days, smile anyway... love anyway.

Teaching is about so much more than just covering standards or a set curriculum. Whatever subject area you teach, make that your passion. Regardless of what age students you teach, being a passionate teacher is going to make a difference. Act silly, laugh, and most importantly, build strong relationships with your students. Students will see and know your passion for your area of teaching!

When your passion and your purpose combine and collide, that is when the magic happens!! I encourage you to walk in your purpose! Know that you are making a difference and the impact that you will have on the lives of your students and generations to come is something that some people never get to experience in a lifetime. And we, as educators have the opportunity to do just that EVERY DAY! Do not take that lightly. Know that you

DOI: 10.4324/9781003216988-29

are a life changer and that what you do and how you do it make a difference!

In the field of education, when you walk in your purpose and do so with a passion, you may not always be understood or liked by those you work with. But guess what, that doesn't matter! And it's okay, you aren't there for them; you are there to make a difference in the lives of your students! Do not lose focus on that or let anyone dull your shine. Shine anyway, love anyway, care anyway, be you anyway, and be who and what your students need.

Ultimately, it is the relationships that will be built, the passion for your purpose that will be shown, and the love that will be shared that will make a difference in the lives of your students. Go forth and make a difference. You matter, what you do matters, and most importantly, the difference that you make and will continue to make matters!

From one life changer to another with love,

Lacey J. Davis
Early Childhood & Elementary Virtual Teacher
Chieftain Virtual Learning Center
Seminole, Oklahoma

One Small Footprint—
One Huge Impact

30

Dear Teacher,

You have the best and the most important job that anyone can wish or hope to experience in their lives. Why do I believe this? The passion, the effort, the drive cannot be stronger than that of a teacher. Today, and every day you are making an impact without even realizing it. I have watched you grow and I know there are times you are working so hard to help make a difference for someone. Yes, there is content being taught by you, but there is so much more than that. You are giving kids and adults alike your very best to help them improve or see some successes. Starting with a smile, the extra encouragement, the belief in them, the hope, the passion, and just showing up every day to be their accountability, that is what makes you become the difference-maker for them, and YOU keep showing up to rally for them! I can say that no two days, the students, or even the years are the same, but each one holds a special place in your heart and somehow there is always room for more. When you are faced with a challenge, look back to your first year teaching or even your first day, or few weeks; remember, you have made it through so much and you will look back and realize it was not so bad. You may even get a good chuckle at the situation, or smile as it is now a happy memory to look back and reflect on.

There are many educators out there that teach for 30+ years, so you can too if that's what you want to do! Either way, you will always remember what you taught others and what others have taught you. We truly are blessed with having something to be poured into others from our hearts and cups, even when we think there is no more left to give. This is when the magic that

DOI: 10.4324/9781003216988-30

you have begins to happen! Please know that your small footprint in your school makes a huge impact in the future! My first students have now blossomed into adults in the world and I can proudly say I helped them become who they are today and who they will become tomorrow. What other profession can say that? You are marvelous, incredible, fantastic, brilliant, and amazing! I believe in you!

Your Biggest Fan,

Lauren Almanza, Principal
La Grange, Texas

A Star is Born—Let Your Little Light Shine!

31

Dear Teacher,

The ESSENTIAL question that I believe a teacher should ask him/herself is: "DID I CHOOSE TEACHING OR DID IT CHOOSE ME?"

You might ask "Why is that question so essential?" Let me explain. I believe that everyone is born with at least one gift in which he/she is to gift the world. Teaching may be that gift; therefore we were chosen for it.

If teaching is not your God-given gift and you choose it, you might not last long in the profession and if you do, it will not bring the joy that it was meant to bring. You may not last long due to several factors, a few of which are: a salary which is not commensurate with many other professions, possible student discipline challenges, lack of parental support, and diminishing appreciation and respect for the profession.

On the other hand, if teaching chose you (inborn gift or "calling") those challenges are overshadowed by the many benefits such as: fulfilling student–teacher relationships, job security – you can move anywhere in the world and find a teaching position waiting for you, and what other profession has the number of vacation days as teachers do?

And let's not forget that teaching is full of little everyday joys from the GENUINENESS of children to the funny things they say and do which energize and enrich our daily lives.

In conclusion, take pride in your profession knowing that you truly touch the lives of many and that your love for what you do will be a light to shine upon all that you encounter.

DOI: 10.4324/9781003216988-31

In my opinion, after several decades in this profession, there is little else more satisfying in life than to hear students say, "You are my favorite teacher!" So please tell yourself everyday –

"I AM A TEACHER AND AM PROUD OF IT!!!"

Marilyn Lunnon
English Teacher
Houston, TX

Now, Go Light Some Fires!

32

Dear Teacher,

If we were in the same room right now I would hug you. I would hug you because I would want you to know how deeply I appreciate the fact that you CHOSE to join this wonderful profession – a profession that will give you intense joy, immense heartache, weary feet, deeply furrowed brows, and a continual warmth like an ember from a fire. The ember will sometimes feel like it's almost extinguished, but I promise you, it never goes all the way out. Sometimes the fire will burn brightly and you'll have to shade your eyes from the light and wipe the tears away that come from seeing things too brightly and beautifully. And some days the cold will creep in and you'll believe the fire to be gone. You will shiver and pull into yourself and wonder if it will ever feel warm and lovely again. But it will, Teacher, and when you were not prepared for this to be the day, you will be gifted a look, or a touch, or a smile, or a drawn picture, or a concept learned, or a vision of someone whose fire is even more nearly extinguished than yours. And this is why I would hug you.

I would want you to know from someone who has been in our profession for a very long time that despite all the nonsense, the changing social climate, the governmental bureaucratic oversight, the lack of personal power and the immensity of personal power, that you will never in any other profession feel so keenly that what you did changed a life profoundly. Someone will come into your classroom not being able to read and you will unlock that treasure for them. Someone will come into your classroom and not be able to connect ideas into a cogent thought that changes the trajectory of their ideas, and you will light that fuse. Someone will come into your classroom feeling like maybe nobody really

DOI: 10.4324/9781003216988-32

cares if they succeed or fail. And you will give them some of those embers you carry around with you as if to say, "I want you to be warm too." And that will start that fire inside of them... and who knows? Maybe someday they will join our wonderful profession and share the light with others. So thank you Teacher, here's your hug. Now go out and light some fires.

With my sincere love and appreciation,

Martin Silverman, Principal
San Antonio, Texas

Be the Teacher YOU Would Want

Dear Teacher,

The job that we do is not for everybody. I truly believe that people have been put on this earth to be teachers and one of those people is YOU! Never lose that willingness to learn and try something new with your students. It is in these moments so many times where memories are made. Don't be afraid to transform that room. Don't be afraid to be silly. Don't be afraid to try something new with your students. Some of my absolute greatest memories are from the times I tried something new and outside of my comfort zone.

One of my years teaching, we were learning about the Oregon Trail. I divided my class into groups, and they had to complete different activities as they went along their journey on the Oregon Trail. We transformed the room and every day stayed in character as we learned many of the hardships that were faced by so many. Students to this day bring up the lesson! They learned a lot and enjoyed doing it at the same time. The nights leading up to the lesson I was nervous, because I was afraid that for some reason it might not work out. In this case it turned out AMAZING!

I can tell you though, not all my lessons are a hit. Some fail and some fail big! Those lessons that don't work out just make you a stronger teacher in the end though. Never be afraid to try something for the fear that it might not work. As long as what you are doing is in the best interest of your students, that is all that matters.

If we expect our students to push themselves and not be afraid of failure, we must do the same. Although it can be easy to get stuck in a rut, we know we must get out of our comfort

DOI: 10.4324/9781003216988-33

zone because our kids deserve it! If we aren't looking forward to the lesson for the next day, how do we think our kids are going to feel?!

I've been in situations where I felt stuck and didn't know how to get out. I needed some positivity and people who could uplift and support me. There are times where you might not be able to find that positivity and uplifting spirit right around you in your school building. Something that really helped me during those times was turning to my Twitter PLN (Professional Learning Network). I would log on and see all sorts of great ideas and people really motivating me to show up each and every day for my students. I have recommended to many teachers to build their PLN. It has helped me during some of my toughest times in teaching when I felt a little lost or like a failure in some way.

Lastly, never underestimate the value of building those relationships with students. Spend time building those relationships with your students. Get to know them and truly care about them. We all know that students learn best from teachers they like, and we really know that students have one of the best radars to be able to tell if a teacher really likes them or not. Every child deserves someone who believes in them and pushes them to be their best.

Ultimately, if you put what is best for kids at the forefront of everything you do, you'll do great!

Keep Living the Dream!

Melinda Cave
8th Grade Teacher/Coach
Rosenberg, Texas

The Answer is Yes!

34

Dear Teacher,

You are exceptional. You are amazing. You are so incredibly amazing that you decided to enter into a profession that creates all the other professions. You have decided to enter a profession in which you make 1,500 educational decisions per day. Just wow. One of those many decisions is probably tied to building relationships with students – just remember the answer is yes. Yes, relationships matter. They matter each and every day.

The yes is the answer to all your relationship wondering questions. Do positive relationships matter with students? The answer is yes. Does it matter more than the content you are actually teaching students? The answer is yes. Can relationships break down walls and make hard conversations easier? The answer is emphatically, "Yes!" We know that's probably not what you expected to read, but we just handed you a major key. Relationships are the foundation of the work that you do with students. They are the foundational work you do with families. Relationships are the foundation to the work you do each and every day. Relationships do matter.

Making connections with others is one way to begin building the foundation of your relationships. Without connections relationships aren't built. However, relationships cannot be built without connections. Did we just blow your mind? We thought so. Creating opportunities to make connections will be key to the work you do each day. It doesn't matter what level of teacher you are or what content area you teach. Creating space for connection-making should happen within your class(es). Without these connections, your relationships with students won't thrive.

Some examples of connection-making with students are: greeting them at the door, holding class meetings, creating

DOI: 10.4324/9781003216988-34

meaningful journaling assignments, sharing life experiences, one-on-one check-ins with students or reading and discussing a good ol' children's book (yup even in middle and high school). This will help in connection-making with your students. This is not an exhaustive list; however, it will begin the process. As Rita Pierson very eloquently stated in her TED talk entitled, "Every Kid Needs a Champion", "You know kids don't learn from people they don't like." It's true. That is why relationships will always come first – even before content. Are we saying that content isn't important – definitely not. However, if the relationship isn't built or at least being built, the content being taught will go in one ear and out the other.

When we think of the teachers that we remember most we think less about what they taught us, but rather how the teachers connected with us, poured into us and valued us as human beings. We think of the teachers that actually "saw" us. The teacher that told us we could do it, told us that they believed in us, told us not to forget about them when we went off to change the world. Those are the teachers that we remember and hold near and dear to our hearts. It does not matter, nor do we remember, the content they taught us. We are sure they taught us something; however, what we took with us was them pouring into us. What we took with us was their belief in us and the connections we made during our time with these rock star teachers. The connections that were built remained. Even though years and years have passed, we remember the relationship that the teacher built with us – those connections remain even after we have moved on.

We are not saying that every relationship that you begin to build will be easy. Some of the building will be backbreaking work. Sometimes connections will be missed and it won't always be your fault. However, you gotta try to connect with your students, try to see them, try to get to know them and show them that you care... even when they've worked your last nerve, even when you're their least favorite person, even when you'd rather run into oncoming traffic during rush hour... Connections lead to relationships; those relationships are the foundation that will carry you through your career as a professional educator. Let the journey begin, you got this!

Best wishes,

Michael & Nita Creekmore

Michael E. Creekmore, Jr. LPC, CPCS
Professional School Counselor/ Licensed Professional Counselor
Loganville, GA

Nita Creekmore
Instructional Coach/Educational Consultant
Loganville, GA

Ready, Set, Teach!

35

Dear Teacher,

It is so exciting and extremely rewarding to be part of such a noble profession. Whether you are just beginning this journey or if you have been on it for decades, it is my hope that you still find the excitement, and especially the love, that first attracted you to the world of education. You probably will never know exactly how many lives you influence every day, how often you are a substitute parent or counselor, and yes, how often you have been or will be the "ATM" for some needy student.

During my five decades of teaching, I think I encountered almost every situation for which there had been no university education or preparation classes. I had to wing it and so will you, especially in this age of technology, negative social media, active shooter lockdown drills, and now a pandemic. Don't give up! You are stronger and smarter than you may think you are, and with personal conduct beyond reproach you will handle each situation with amazing courage and phenomenal grace. And don't forget that sense of humor. When all the educational madness is swirling around you, that sense of humor will be your shield.

Decades ago, I read the following "advertisement" in "The Reader's Digest", and I can tell you from personal experience, it is rather funny and quite true:

Wanted: Teachers

"Must have the wisdom of Solomon, the courage of David and the patience of Job.

Must be able to lead like Moses, teach like St. Paul, and stay cool under fire like Shadrach."

DOI: 10.4324/9781003216988-35

YOU undoubtedly qualify! Congratulations! You got the job!

Patricia (Pat) Bonner
Kinder High School for the Performing and Visual Arts Music
    Dept. (ret.)
Houston, Texas

Dear Irreplaceable Teacher

36

Dear Teacher,

Where do I begin to express how important the role you play in the lives of kids actually is! It seems most days you are tasked with the impossible: reaching every child's individual learning style, moving them forward in performance levels, meeting all their social/emotional needs, teaching them right from wrong, providing them a moral compass, all on limited time and budgets. When you sit and think about what is expected in a day's time, it's daunting. As daunting as it may be, you remain steadfast, you remain constant and you remain dedicated. Why, one may ask; it's because you, the educator, understand a child's needs and see the potential that every child possess. You see the "Big Picture" and know that you alone may be the best adult guidance a child receives on their journey in life.

Many do not understand the life of an educator. They think it's an easy road with summer off and long holidays! We chuckle at this notion because we know the responsibility we carry as educators. It's the weight of the world... it actually is! When times get tough, things get crazy, you feel like you can't go on... that's when you stop, take a deep breath and dig in! The quality and meaning you alone can bring to a child's life is worth every hard day! Never doubt your worth or your value! Never give up on being an advocate for children and fighting for them to have opportunities, whatever they may be! Imagine life without the educator... YES, you are that important!

With admiration and praise,

Rachel M. Crider
Chief Elementary Instructional Officer
Floyd County Schools

DOI: 10.4324/9781003216988-36

Just the Way You Are

37

Dear Teacher,

> You are enough. Just as you are.
> So are your students. Just as they are.
>
> You are all doing your best.
> Your best is always changing.
> Whether it feels like "enough," it is no less your best.
>
> "Enough" is an elusive standard.
> Life has become an extreme sport.
> There is so much pressure to perform and so little grace
>   for being human.
>
> Shame, judgment, and pushing won't help you or your
>   students do better or feel like "enough." Compassion,
>   empathy, and grace will.
>
> "Enough" comes from meeting yourself and your
>   students exactly where you are and honoring
>   yourselves for exactly who you are.
>
> "Enough" comes from you and your students feeling
>   seen, heard, and understood.
>
> "Enough" comes from building on your own and your
>   students' unique strengths.
>
> That is the curriculum of life. Meet people where they
>   are. Honor them for who they are. Help them feel
>   seen, heard, and understood. Build on their strengths
>   to help them grow.

DOI: 10.4324/9781003216988-37

That's what teachers and students need to teach and
learn to be successful professionals, partners, parents,
and people of the world.

The magic of education, for teachers and students, is
being empowered, feeling deeply, and truly knowing
that you are "enough."

You are enough. Just as you are. And so are your
students. Just as they are.

From my heart to yours,

Rebecca A. Weiner, M.Ed.
Educational Consultant & Creator of Learn Play Grow
Houston, Texas, USA and all over the interwebs

You Gave Me the World   38

Dear Teacher,

You need to know the impact that you had on my world. I chose the word WORLD and not LIFE because life implies "just me," and what you did for me was so much greater than that. You impacted my WORLD! You saw in me potential that was far greater than what I saw in myself, and honestly you saw in me what others did not. You were the one that made me believe that I could do more, learn more, and achieve more.

I wasn't the smartest student sitting in your classroom, but you were amazingly gifted in making me believe that I could be the smartest student in your classroom. You let me know that you believed in me; you instilled in me the confidence to believe in myself. I know the extra time you took to re-teach a concept to me, and I understand you were burning valuable minutes that you would never recoup, but by taking those extra minutes, you showed me that you weren't giving up on me, that I was worth your time. You listened to me when I needed someone to hear me. You were kind to me when I needed kindness. You were a smile and an encouraging word when I was feeling sad. You understood that even when we weren't learning the lessons in your lesson plans for the day, we were still learning about life, about the WORLD, by being in your classroom. There are no words, song lyrics, or verses that can convey the gratitude I have for your investment in me. I remember one day leaving your classroom and thinking, "My teacher thinks I am worth the time. My teacher believes in me." WOW!

Teacher, oh how I wish I would have had the courage, words, maturity, and emotional capacity to have said to you at the time how important your work was. What a difference you were making in the world, in MY world. How your investment would pay dividends multiplied by so many lives you touched as you

DOI: 10.4324/9781003216988-38

graced the door of the classroom each day. When you opened the door of your classroom, you opened my mind and you opened my heart. You gave me a piece of yourself that I will carry with me always. Today is the day, the day I want you to know how important you are. Your love for teaching and learning always showed. I never doubted that you were an expert. In my eyes, you knew it all, and I wanted to be just like you!

Teacher, as you lay your head on your pillow tonight... as you languish over the struggling child in your classroom... as you worry about the one that will go to bed hungry... as you second guess your instructional strategies... as you wonder how you will get all of the boxes checked in the next day... don't! Never worry that you are not enough, that you are not doing enough, giving enough. The fact that you worry about being a good teacher is what makes you a great one. Rest in the grace of patience to yourself. Rest in knowledge that you filled the hours of the day with good stuff for your students. Rest with courage to face the next day. JUST REST... students need you, the world needs you.

Appreciatively,

Rhonda Turner
Superintendent of Schools Quitman ISD
Quitman, Texas

Look for the God Winks. They Are There!

39

Dear Teacher,

There was a time, within every community, where two professions operated with unmatched reverence and respect. Two professions that many viewed as the linchpins of a successful community. Two professions that fathers and mothers gloated with pride if their sons/daughters chose to pursue. These professions: the priesthood and education, seemingly operated with divine providence!

Since the onset of humanity, our teachers were the purveyors of knowledge that society deemed "essential". Teachers had the burden, and honor, of passing along the "truth" from one generation to the next. Without teachers, communities would not endure. Without teachers, future generations would falter.

I chose to open up my letter in this manner to let you know that YOU, an educator, are valued, and have been since the beginning. Though it may sometimes seem like the praise and respect our society doles out to our profession is at an all-time low, I want you to know that you ARE vital to the success of our world! You are still loved. You were placed by a higher power, wherever you are reading this, for a particular reason.

I want to challenge you, daily, to look for the #godwinks. Look for evidence that you are EXACTLY in the right spot, at EXACTLY the right time. Look for evidence that you are revered. Look for evidence that ours is still a divine profession. I promise you, take the time to look, because they are there!

In closing, thank you. Thank you for coming into the building every day prepared to change the world. Thank you for being the best hope of improving our world. Thank you for believing

DOI: 10.4324/9781003216988-39

in the divinity of our profession and being optimistic enough to ignore the nay-sayers!!!

You are amazing!

Ryan Scott
Webster County High School
Assistant Principal
Dixon, Kentucky

Magic in the Chaos

40

Dear Teacher,

I never planned on becoming a teacher. In fact, I was pretty bitter about it. I would scoff at aspiring teachers and boast "I would never do so much for so little." I mean, kudos to me for realizing this profession is a lot of work, but wow, what a brat I was.

I would like to tell you that I snapped out of that mindset after the first few days and traded in my bitterness for a sweater covered in embroidered school buses and apples. But that is far from the truth. It took three years. I never bought the sweater, but I did fall in love with teaching.

There's something magical about the routine and the chaos. I love that I can be sure at least one kid every day will compliment something about my outfit. I love that I can be unsure of when the fire alarm will go off. I love the assurance that seeing a student in public will result in meeting every family member they are with. I love the chaos of a holiday classroom party.

But there will be times you will be so unsure of yourself. I was so convinced that I wasted those first three years and that my students felt cheated.

The students I taught then did not get the best of my teaching, which I felt so much guilt about. I shared this with a former student a few years after I moved on to another school and felt more joy than I felt I deserved in that job. She looked at me with a shocked expression and quickly replied "that was not my experience at all." From her perspective, I was fun and eager. While I felt like I was only a day ahead of students with the curriculum, she never knew it. I was pure chaos, and she loved it.

It felt as if someone lifted huge chains off of me. The guilt, shame, and bitterness melted away. I came to an important

DOI: 10.4324/9781003216988-40

realization that day – you cannot be a perfect teacher, but your students don't expect or want you to be. They want you to be authentically you.

Teaching is a journey. We grow and evolve every year. The beautiful part is that we don't carry our mistakes or shortcomings into a new year. Our students don't hold on to any negative memories of where we didn't quite measure up. What do they remember? They remember when we laugh with them. They remember every time we showed them grace, every hug, every kind note. They remember our hearts – not our grasp of curriculum or teaching strategies.

And we remember theirs. I remember the students who pooled their money to buy me flowers after my grandfather died. I remember the student who had her mom make me a sandwich every day for lunch because she knew that is my favorite food and her mom was exceptionally good at making sandwiches. I remember the student who bought me an American Girl doll when I casually mentioned in class how I always wanted one as a kid. I remember the student who made my coffee every morning and talked about life with me. I remember the student who messaged me every day of sorority rush to keep me updated on the journey.

I do not remember any failed quizzes or missed assignments. My students are not clothed in their mistakes when I remember them. I remember them by their humor, their kindness, their passions, their sarcasm, etc.

And they will remember you the same. They will remember how you like your coffee. They will think of you when walking through the candy section during the holidays. They will sit around with classmates and talk about how much you mean to them. They will send you graduation announcements and wedding invitations. You will watch them marry the loves of their lives and they will rush to introduce you to that special person to you as another special person in their life.

Stay the course. Dig in and give love out in large doses. Never be afraid to admit defeat or own mistakes. In times when you feel your attitude is all off, show gratitude and watch it shift your mood.

You are loved. You are important. You are so needed.
Go get 'em and buy the yearbook.

Samantha Jo Berry
Journalism adviser
Bridgeland High School
Cypress, Texas

Find Your Village and See the Good

41

Dear Teacher,

You may be reading this letter on a good day. Everything is going great. You even remembered to turn your attendance in on time and no one had to call and remind you!! But maybe it's not a good day. Maybe you spent the drive to work wondering how you could even make it through the day. There are so many things on your plate. Every one of us is carrying a plate piled high with expectations, responsibilities, and sometimes deep personal pain. Your struggles may be different from mine but we are all pushing through, day after day. Then you get to school and the struggles of home/family/relationships/finances have to get put on hold for a while. You have a completely different set of struggles when you enter the halls of your school.

We always hear the phrase "It takes a village to raise a child." Usually the focus is on the child in the context of what is being said, but to me the key word in that phrase is *"village."* Find your village!! Other teachers who you can count on to encourage and uplift you! Care for one another! Look for ways to lift one another up through encouragement and kind words. Find ways to influence your school climate for the better. Take care of each other and let others take care of you. So many times people offer to "help" and it may be hard to let them. Let people in. Let them carry you when you need to be carried.

You have to find the right balance. The balance that keeps you healthy. Healthy both physically and mentally. You cannot always be "ON"! It is not sustainable. I am always telling my students "Kindness Matters" and it does, but we have to remember to be kind to ourselves also!! We are so quick to give grace to others but then we turn around and beat ourselves up

DOI: 10.4324/9781003216988-41

over the smallest things. Dear friend, you deserve the grace that you so freely give to others!!

You must practice self-care. I know this topic isn't always a popular one. In our field, it is seen as heroic to work and engage as much as humanly possible, but the truth is there comes a point where self-care matters and is just as important. You have to know it is ok to have some boundaries over your time. It is ok to not stay at school until late evening all the time. It is ok to not bring huge bags stuffed with all the grading and planning home every evening. It is ok to be human. Plan your days and weeks as purposely balanced as possible. Also have checks and balances in your routines with other educators. We are in this together.

Are Mondays hard for you? Or maybe Thursday is the day you think you just can't make it another day? Set a calendar "event" on your phone that repeats every week on that day! A note of encouragement just for you! A reminder that you've got this! Because YOU DO! You can do the hard things! We are educators! We are innovative, we are flexible, we are resourceful and we are resilient! We have proven this time and time again.

I know to hear the media and outside influences, one might think education as a whole needs to be completely revamped. I don't agree with this. Yes, there are issues needing to be addressed and fixed but these people are not with us day in and day out. They are not seeing the impact you are making. There are truly life-changing things happening in classrooms every day. They are happening in your classroom! Look for that good!

Thank YOU for making me curious about how others do the same thing I do and helping me see ways to do it better. You motivate me. You push me to be a better teacher and I thank you.

Tammi Halliburton
5th grade Teacher
Orange, Texas

My Love

42

Dear Teacher,

I have hundreds of stories to tell you that are heartwarming success stories, but what I want to tell you to start off is how you get those stories. It sounds strange but you can't take anything personal. All my stories become personal but I couldn't take them personally at the time. I had to be the adult. I had to be consistent. I couldn't let my feelings get hurt or think about my feelings at all. I didn't get to have a bad day no matter what was going on in my life. When a student came to see me they saw the same person every time. They heard the same answers, saw the same expectations. They felt safe. They learned to trust.

The hardest kid I ever mentored is now like a son to me. I didn't know when to be hard or when to be soft. But I never gave up. He was eight of nine children. No one in his family had ever graduated from high school. He was an extraordinary athlete but his walls were up and they weren't coming down. Once you got to know him, he was an extraordinary young man. Honest, kind, thoughtful, funny but he didn't want anyone to know that. We went through hurdles together but I always stayed calm, consistent, honest, caring. Long story short, that young man – the one everyone knew was going to be a high school dropout – graduated from high school. He set the tone. Number nine had no choice but to graduate. And all his nieces and nephews now saw a different story. Could choose a different path. The ripple effect. He will always be a part of my life and my family's life and that makes me so happy.

Another student was so angry and rude. I never let him disrespect me. But I let him try to work through some of the anger. When he graduated, I felt we had some moments but I wasn't sure I had reached him. Three years after he graduated, he came back to school to apologize to me for being rude. He said I was always so kind to him but he had lots of issues and he wanted to

DOI: 10.4324/9781003216988-42

thank me for my kindness and not giving up on him. You reach kids even if you don't think you are. He explained to me that my kindness but toughness helped him stick it out to graduate. As he got in the real world and matured and looked at life differently, he was embarrassed about his behavior. He wanted to come back and let me know that I had gotten through to him even when it looked like I hadn't.

One of my students hated school. He was so angry with teachers, coaches and administration. He was a hot head but in my mind, he was still a student. We were the adults. We had to make sure he felt validated in some way. He was never disrespectful to me. He would come in my office red as a beet he would be so mad. But he had learned that if he didn't pop off at the teachers that I could help him. He learned to come to my office to cool off. He didn't walk on graduation and told me he would never come back to school. When I retired, he showed up at my retirement party. He made my day. I knew it was so hard for him to come back in the building. I was honored that he did that for me.

Like I said, I have hundreds of stories that are examples of why we do what we do. I love telling my stories. I am so blessed that so many kids (now grownups) are still a part of my life. They take a moment to reach out and check on me and I am overwhelmed with gratitude and love. But that doesn't just happen. I am so lucky that I know why I was put on this Earth. I am so blessed that I got to be a part of these students' lives. I couldn't wait to get back after the weekend or a holiday to check on my kids. I knew that a lot of them had not been hugged or shown attention since we left. Kids need to be loved. They need to be hugged. We are all adults; we know how to hug a child so that they feel the love but it is not inappropriate. Don't let that be your excuse. I also use words of endearment. I'm from Texas. I'm from the South. We honey baby each other and don't even know it. One day this kid (a very tough kid) came in my office and said "Sometimes I just try to get in trouble to come in your office." I said, "Let's work out a deal where you can come visit me if you haven't been in trouble." Lol. He also told me that he loved to come to see me to hear me call him "my love". I didn't know that

I even called him that but it was something that made him feel loved, important, validated. Just the little things.

So, dear teacher, just be you. Understand that the small things you do like listening, being consistent, smiling, laughing are the things that will make the success stories. I love the stories I have. I love the people who will always be a part of my life because of our connection when they were students. I am so thankful that I got to do what God put me on this Earth to do. Go make your success stories and have fun doing it. Thank you for your service.

xo,

Mama Rocc

Tara Roccaforte
Retired Principal's Secretary/Promoted to Gangy
Klein, TX

Keep Taking the Next Step

43

Dear Teacher,

I know it can be hard, and even impossible sometimes. There is so much to do and so many things that need your attention. I get it. I've been there. Some days we feel like we can conquer the world, and other days we feel like it is conquering us. I need you to know that no matter what kind of day today is, you are helping someone conquer their world today. You are the difference in someone's day today. You are the reason someone will show up and show out today.

I know you are strong. How do I know? There is no way to do what we do with that inner strength. I know you are brave. How? You step into the unknown each day and help guide the lives of so many young people each and every day.

You see, when you think about it, you are really a superhero. You create everything the world needs. You support every area of success and create the future every single day. You are the one making the world we have been dreaming of one class at a time. Adults will think of you for the rest of their lives and be so thankful that you started them on the road they went down. You were the turning point of their lives to help guide them exactly where they needed to be.

I have always said that if I can move a student an inch to the left or right today, imagine how far apart their futures will be. That is you today. You are creating that difference in their lives.

I'm not saying that there won't be rough times. It will get hard from time to time. Don't let it get you down. Turn the obstacles into an opportunity today. Show your staff and students just how you can use that. Just because you run into a detour, that does not mean that it is the end of your journey. It just means you

DOI: 10.4324/9781003216988-43

need to find a way around. I have had more detours than I can remember, but each and every one led me to where I am now.

I started as a bus driver and volunteer coach. I moved to teacher, then specialist, coordinator, director, and have done a little of it all. Every bit of it taught me something. I'm here to tell you that you are no different. Your role means nothing in the scheme of things. It's what you do with the role you are given that makes the difference.

Little and big eyes watch you every day. I know I get energized by other educators all the time. Their drive, their heart, and their understanding push me to be better every day. You see it isn't just the students you inspire. Those around you are in awe of you as well. Do not sell yourself short. You are a world changer. You don't have to change the whole world, but if you help one person, you have changed their entire world.

Sincerely,

Taylor Armstrong
Executive Director Of Technology/CIO at
Hinds Community College
Raymond, Mississippi

The ABCs of a Teacher

Dear Teacher,

T is for **TOUCH**. Just think of all those lives you are going to touch in your lifetime. Hundreds. Perhaps thousands. What a special career you chose! YOU get to be a special part in the lives of each student that you encounter. Not just those you teach, but all those students that you see every single day. A little piece of you will always live in them. Make it count. I came upon the following quote early in my teaching career. It is questionable where the quote originated, but I would still like to share it with you here – "I've learned that people will forget what you said, people will forget what you did, but people will never forget how you made them feel." How DO you want to make your students feel? How do you want to touch their lives? You are so important.

E is for **ENERGY**. I'm not talking about being "energetic" by jumping up and down and shouting when you are teaching. I'm talking about a dynamic type of energy. The type of energy that you get when talking about something you love. Do you love teaching? Do you love what you teach? Do you feel a spark inside you when you are sharing that knowledge with your students? That spark is the energy I'm talking about. That spark is why we teach. As I'm sharing this with you, I'm feeling that spark. That energy. It makes me excited about writing to you. I'm not exhausted when I've been teaching all day, I'm energized because I've been teaching something that I love. Having that spark is something special. Share your spark.

A is for **All In**. My wonderful drama professor would always let us know when we were "phoning it in" regarding a performance. What he meant was that we were on automatic and just saying words and not believing what we were saying. Phoning it in is the easy way out when you are sharing knowledge that

DOI: 10.4324/9781003216988-44

you've shared over and over again. But if you have that spark that I mentioned, you will go from phoning it in to being ALL IN! Give it your all, all the time. 100%. And remember that your "all" may be different from day to day and that is okay. Sometimes things happen in our lives and we think, "How can I go into that classroom and teach when 'blank' is happening in my life?" We are human. You can still be all in. You can still give 100%. It is 100% of you in that moment in time. All in – all the time.

C is for **Channel**. I'm guessing that one of the reasons you ended up being a teacher is because you had a special teacher (or maybe many special teachers) who inspired you. On those days when you feel you can't be "all in," that's the time to channel those special teachers that you had. They are there for you now, just like they were there for you then. Let them be your guides to get you through the not so smooth times. Think WWMSTD? (What would my special teacher do?) My 5th grade teacher, Mr. Sarasin, was my "ST." He let me be me. He encouraged my creativity and was an integral part of shaping who I am today. And to this day, 50 years later, I hear his voice of encouragement and I channel him in my teaching. Isn't it wonderful to wonder who will be hearing your voice 50 years from now?

H is for **Heart**. It hasn't been scientifically proven, but I am sure of it – teachers have XXL hearts. Can't you feel it? Doesn't your heart swell when you see students learn something that you taught them? Doesn't your heart swell even more when those students apply what you taught them to something else and they come up with their own ideas? It's surprising that our hearts even fit into our chests after teaching year after year. And what about that love that we feel for those students who we know need extra love. Our hearts NEED to be XXL so we can spread our love to our students throughout our entire teaching career. I can hear the beating of your XXL heart all the way from here.

E is for **Extra**. In addition to your extra, extra-large heart, there is so much more "extra" to mention! Most important, you are EXTRA special. You are extra special for choosing to be a teacher. You are extra special for going that extra mile, even when you thought you didn't have it in you. You are extra special for all those extra hours you put in. You are extra special for making so many students feel extra special. You are extra special for all the extras you bring into your teaching in so many ways. You are EXTRAordinary.

R is for **Radiant**. I had so many possible choices for "R" and I'm smiling as I write because the word I settled on is perfect. Remember those special teachers I spoke of earlier? Another of my special teachers is Miss Fredricks, my 3rd grade teacher. Every Friday she would read a chapter of Charlotte's Web to us. Charlotte wove "radiant" into her web to describe Wilber. Isn't it fitting that in looking for an "R" word to describe what a teacher is, I chose a word that I learned from one of my favorite teachers? And the definition of "radiant" is "sending out rays of light." That's exactly what teachers do – we extend our rays to enlighten. You are radiant. Feel yourself radiating as you teach – now and always.

Tina Sabuco
Foundress and Artistic Director of Arts Alive! Inc.
Educator for 45 years
Houston, Texas

The Essence of YOU

45

Dear Teacher,

As I write, I'm thinking fondly of your healing smile and your warm intentions. I know you don't know me, but I know you so well. I've treasured you in the deepest part of my heart for many years. You, sweet Teacher, are my very own rescuer of the hopeless. A grounded angel. A keeper and generous supplier of the magical gift of human potential. Although I am now a teacher as well, I'm speaking to you here in the voice of my childhood, as a student who desperately needed you and the goodness you freely share. Then again, I speak to you as a fellow educator who understands your hardships. These two roles make me fully qualified to remind you of what you truly are: A Difference-Maker.

For nearly 10 years, I've worn the prestigious title of educator. I'm living a dream I could have never imagined during my time as a student. Not only did I live in high poverty in the poorest part of the country, but I had suffered a great deal of trauma and carried a 504 Plan with extra accommodations for the legally blind. Although the odds seemed stacked against me, you would soon discover that intelligence and creativity were hidden beneath those thick glasses and second-hand clothes.

Fast forward to the present and here I am today, insanely proud and honored to be addressing this letter to you. It seems that I have somehow transpired through it all to gain the super-human abilities of the heroes I so admire. I am living the bright and joyful future that you swore could exist. Sometimes I still stop and wonder to myself, *How did I come to this wonderful place?* At that point, my heart earnestly reminisces back to YOU.

I'm sure at this point you are humbly sweeping away this immense compliment and insisting that you don't usually make this type of profound influence. With all due respect Teacher, let me remind you that great impact comes from the small, subtle

DOI: 10.4324/9781003216988-45

choices and relationships of the everyday, of which you are a master. Here are some of the seemingly ordinary, yet miraculous things you do daily that have changed my life and the lives of every child you serve.

*You smile (like **all** the time).* Although it's a simple gesture, your relentless smile is an invaluable gift. My six-year-old self gawked at you continually, wondering how you could be so happy. Your glow was healing and could make me forget my hurt in an instant. It made me wonder if there was some sort of destiny beyond a home life shattered by alcoholism. Could *I find a life that made me smile this way?* Year after year, I found more and more of those smiles and it fed my goals for the future. Through your smiling face, students see hope and a wonderful model of joy. Never underestimate its small but mighty power.

You see the good. You look past the evident and find competence in children – and they revel in your discoveries. Despite my reality of being moved from home to home and sometimes shelter-to-shelter, you saw my love for writing and the pride I felt at being praised. I was more than a legally blind child living off the streets; I had hidden talents that could help me escape my presumed fate. You helped me find many treasures within, of which I cling to, even to this day. Just by pointing out strengths, you give other students that same endowment. It fuels their little hearts and sparks visions of what is possible.

You create safety. The atmosphere you provide all students is a sanctuary many couldn't bear to do without. In many instances, your classroom was the only promise I could count on during dark moments of fear. In the midst of a psychotic rage of an abusive step-father, comfort was found in knowing that within a few short hours my teacher would be expecting me. No matter how ridden by hunger or fear, I could soon enjoy the feasts of the school lunchroom and return to the fortress of my classroom desk. You were always there, an unknowing ally when the rest of life was in turmoil and ruin. Thank you for creating a safe haven for me and for all of your students; it's unlikely you'll ever fully understand just how incredible it is.

You show up every day. I hope you realize this is most crucial of all the duties that you hold. It is this reliability and repetition that provides all of the other bounties I've mentioned. As a teacher, I now realize how difficult and trying this part of your career can be. Returning day after day to a position that is sometimes thankless, unappreciated and overwhelming is a noble contribution to the greater good. On tired days, emotionally trying days and even on sick days, you show up for your kids and I'm thanking you deeply for that. By showing up for me, you gave me the power to overcome disability, neglect, abuse and the powerful hold of learned helplessness that promised to be my fate. Remember that I am only one of the thousands you have (or will) impact over your career. You are a big deal, my friend.

I hope by reading this message of sincere gratitude, you recognize that these are all qualities you possess. Recognize them and stand firm in them. Your value to the world isn't in meticulous lesson planning, headache-inducing data tracking or any of the burdensome tasks that we put so much pressure on ourselves to get right. Your value to children is simply YOU and all the subtle actions you, as an incredible human being, do naturally. The only thing you need to do now is simply… keep on doing them.

Many blessings to you, from one of your greatest admirers.

Teacher Toni
Primary Teacher & Content Creator
Litt Carr, Kentucky

Think of Teaching as Facilitating a Purpose

46

Dear Teacher,

Think of teaching as facilitating purpose.

Facilitate = To make it easier
Purpose = Your reason for doing.

Your job is to make it easier for our kids to find and do what they love, and your role is the most unique in a child's life. Each year you spend more time with the kids in your classroom than anybody else in their life. Think about it: 8 hours at school, 8 hours to sleep, and 8 hours for family, friends, and fun.

Growing up, we moved 11 times, and I went to eight schools, but I still remember the teachers who were supportive and demanding to help me reach my potential. Mr. Cooper, Mrs. Offengender, Coach Kasper, Dr. Johnson, Dr. Mark, Coach Searfoss, Mrs. Gandara.

My favorite teachers created opportunities for me and my classmates to grow, lead, and experience. Sometimes the simplest way to do that is a small conversation, a thoughtful compliment, feedback that hits home.

I've heard it said that a spaceship on its way to the moon would miss its mark by 150 million miles if it's off target by just 1°. That's why each ship has a gyroscope that autocorrects the route each time it gets off target just a fraction of a degree.

You are the gyroscope for each student in your classroom; your constant corrections, attention, empathy, and grace are what's going to reach its destination.

During homeroom last year, my students asked all kinds of questions about my favorite subject, experience, and course…

DOI: 10.4324/9781003216988-46

"Mr. Tre, how come you decided to be a teacher? They don't make any money."

The response was easy; "I don't think there's anything more valuable that I can do with my life than serve and prepare the next generation for success."

We should be paid more, and as a whole, we deserve more respect as professionals. But at the end of the day, when you see someone living their dream, it either makes you want to be a part of that dream or start to live your own.

Are you running towards your dream? If so, don't stop! The future needs you.

Tre Gammage
Dean of Students, Adult SEL Consultant
South Carolina

The Choice

47

Dear Teacher,

The general public thinks they know what a teacher does all day in the classroom because, frankly, most people have spent time as students in schools.

But the secret to keep yourself moving forward with soul-searching drive is to IGNORE the general public and lean on like-minded educators who UNDERSTAND the complex nature of your profession.

Choose to shine—be that remarkable, creative, innovative teacher that kindly invites others who do not understand to kindly wear shades—do not dim your light to make others comfortable.

Choose to be authentic and transparent—use your LIFE as a teaching tool. Nothing is off the table. A student, a fellow teacher or a parent needs to hear your story—or a piece of your story to help them move forward to their next chapter.

Choose to CELEBRATE and EMBRACE those moments when students realize their greatness because of you! We don't always see the impact that we have on a child but it's there

Choose to be a role model for students, teachers and parents. Be aware that your choices inside and outside of the classroom, and on social media are being seen, heard and judged.

Our profession—teaching—will be dumbed down to: numbers, stats, state rankings and salacious headlines in the public court of law.

But, recognize that your most important contribution as an educator is the way you uplift, inspire and motivate your students to see beyond their current set of circumstances and challenge them to see themselves, their futures and their world in a more hopeful light, by challenging them to do more than they thought possible.

DOI: 10.4324/9781003216988-47

As a teacher, you are one of the most influential humans in a student's life. The words you choose, the energy you bring, the actions you take—potentially can change lives for the better or the worse.

Choose better!
Choose to be THE ONE who moves a student to take action and change our world.

Tricia Sents Kiah
Camden, New York
Camden Central Schools—Special Education Teacher

On New Perspectives and Second Chances

48

Dear Teacher,

I knew at an early age I wanted to be a "teacher." Adults would ask me what I wanted to be when I grew up; the answer was easy. When I was five, I wanted to be a monkey. By the time I was 12, I wanted to be a teacher. It wasn't until I was in college I understood what being a teacher really meant.

I was a volunteer with the ESL program at the local adult education center. The class was full of recent refugees, and I was clumsily teaching them basic conversational English. I would ask a simple question, and they would respond in kind. "What makes you sad?" I chirped, and modeled a response: "I am sad when it rains and I want to be outside." Simple words, simple compound sentence. I asked the question of the middle-aged man to my left. "What makes you sad?"

He took a moment, searching for the words. Slowly, he spoke. "It makes me sad… when… I move to America and leave my family behind."

Another responded, "It makes me sad when… I was buried under the earth and could not see the sky."

Yet another: "It makes me sad when… my baby was taken from me and I never saw her again."

They looked at me, waiting for me to praise their English. Wanting me to recognize they knew *exactly* what sadness meant. At that moment I understood that I understood so little. That a teacher not only taught her students, but learned from them as well. It is a lesson I have never forgotten, and has shaped me as a teacher and a human ever since.

My philosophy has developed, blossomed, bloomed and changed during my 25 years as a teacher. When I first began teaching, my goals were overly idealistic: "If I can even save

DOI: 10.4324/9781003216988-48

one child…" I have since come to understand that teaching isn't about reaching one child, but stimulating knowledge, interest, and growth in many children. Students don't need saving; they need insight into the human condition and the communication skills to connect to those not only around them but those across the world. They need the knowledge base to allow them to make informed decisions and conscious assessments of the world in which we live.

I firmly believe that students do not learn by only one method; students need to be challenged to think and look at the world in new ways. They need to be problem solvers. They need to have compassion. They can learn as much from each other as they can from me. I need to model these behaviors in my classroom and in my life.

What truly drives my teaching is the students themselves. My reward comes through that amazing moment when they finally "get" it. When they ask a question no one thought of asking before and don't wait for me to give them the answer. They figure it out themselves. They show up in class saying, "Hey! Moore! Did you know we could do this?" and then show me exactly how to do it via TikTok or YouTube or just trying on their own until it works out. They teach me as I teach them. It's a full circle in my classroom, and I love it.

I keep a "Kudos" file of cards and letters from throughout the years that I can flip through when I need to be reminded of why I am a teacher. My favorite is from a boy from years ago I had twice. First time he failed miserably. Shut down. Hated school and hated life. Might have hated me. I knew there was more to him than the front he put up. I had him a second time in summer school, in a small class. I teased him about his tattoos. Made him laugh while I helped him read sentences aloud. Listened when he told me about the divorce. About the drugs. About rehab. He passed that summer class, barely. Two years later, a letter arrived, typed. A thank you for a second chance, the only one he ever got. He said he'd never forget it; I'll never forget him.

As I've been reading for the past few decades, the biggest issues facing education today involve resources, politics, apathy, and accountability. These issues have always been a part of our system; I don't believe I'm being negative to think they always will. I'm not naïve enough to believe there is any educational trend that will come along and fix it all, either.

Perhaps the truest resolution to the issues in education can be summarized in the wisdom of Mahatma Gandhi: *be the change you want to see in the world.*

The bottom line is this: I am a teacher. I can fear the issues and wrap myself up in the perception that my program is underfunded, my parents uninvolved, my students uninterested, my colleagues bitter and my governor... well, never mind.

OR, I can make a very important choice every day when I enter my classroom. I can choose to identify my needs in my subject and work diligently asking the right people the right questions until I find the resources to fund/supply the technology my students deserve. Meanwhile, I teach my kids their creativity is not limited to the year our equipment was built or the gigabytes our computers hold. We research tricks, discover new methods, try and fail and try and fail and build confidence while we do so. We clap for each other when a problem is solved.

I make connections with the parents of my students, through my web page, phone calls, and emails. I send out success stories and ideas to use at home. I involve parents in the process of creating class projects, and understand that not all parents have the time, energy or resources to be active in their child's school career.

I challenge students to think better of themselves and of their peers. To respect creativity, compassion, and thoughtfulness. Students can understand that in the real world, "good enough" rarely is, and that is not a standard we allow in our classroom. I teach them what my mother taught me: only boring people get bored. Have a boring project? Whose fault is that? Take responsibility for what you produce, what you create. Save the complaints for your pillow. Find the problems and fix them. Recognize when to walk away and take a breather. Don't settle.

I opt to surround myself with professionals who, like me, love their job and love being around students. I encourage and uplift the great teachers we have at our school, and let them know how fortunate I feel to work with them. I try to build a community of support with my colleagues, the support staff, and fellow employees of the district. Don't like what's going on at school? Find a way to fix it; complaining hours on end in the staff lounge has rarely resulted in positive growth for anyone. I want to be the change. It's something I work on daily, often stumbling, often falling, but always getting back up again.

Why do I love teaching? Because I understand that I understand so little. Because I believe in second chances. And because I continually allow myself to change, to grow, to learn from those around me on this amazing, crazy journey called life.

Welcome to the club.

Trina Moore
Teacher
Leander, Texas

The Hallway Hero in You   49

Dear Teacher,

We see you. We see all the hard work you put into making sure your students love learning. We see you on the days where you may not be feeling your best but you still manage to show up for us. We see you and your resilience to never give up on us no matter how much we may say we can't or we won't. In those moments where we feel defeated, you smile and tell us how much you believe in us and everything we have managed to accomplish thus far. After that moment and from those moments on we give all we can because you said we could.

My caring teacher, you are the person I look forward to seeing every day. You are the one I aspire to be like. You are the one I want to impress. You are the person I will think about when I feel like I cannot do something. You are the reason I get up every morning. It is you I wish I came home to. It is your voice, strategies, activities, and silly jokes I will remember to tell my own kids when they begin school.

I am not sure you know how important you are to me and so many others. Do you realize that you have the power to make or break my day? You have the ability to create human thinkers and innovators. My dear teacher, you have the capability of allowing me to create the best version of myself. It is because of you I can write, read, and problem solve. It is you that allowed me to use my imagination to create stories, play, and learn all at the same time. It is because of you that I learned from my failures and saw my obstacles as opportunities for growth.

You see my dear teacher, I write these words above to share some hope with you. The experiences above are mine, yours, and future teachers that may come after us. These words are of experiences I had as a student, teacher, and have had the privilege of hearing from past students.

DOI: 10.4324/9781003216988-49

I want you to know that this profession is not for the weak, it never has been. Within this profession, we must set out every day to inspire, motivate, educate, and love every student, every family, every day that we make the choice to show up. As a teacher, you get to create lifelong learners that go out into the world and have the ability to be... well, anything they want to be. You, teacher, must know that this job is more than a job; it is a calling and our students' past, present, and future are counting on you.

Your biggest fan,

Valerie Nesmith-Arechiga
Assistant Principal
Corpus Christi, Texas

What If They Were Yours? **50**

Dear Teacher,

Good morning! It's your first day; maybe it's your first day to your first year or first day to your twenty-fifth year, all in all it is the same. Here you sit with your bags packed, your outfit picked with a purpose, and of course your coffee in your hand. You give yourself a glance in your review mirror to give yourself that last boost of confidence you need before facing twenty-plus students. As you slowly creep out of your car to start making your way towards the school building you begin rehearsing your opening speech to your students in your head; possibly even inserting a motivational quote here and there that you remember googling beforehand. Then, before you know it, you have made it to your room to start overly preparing for the day.

What's that? Is that some shuffling feet you hear approaching your way? You look up and see that your first few students have arrived. You stand a little taller and muster up a few words to greet them. They eat up what you have to say with a smile and excitement in their steps as they head to their seats. At this point you are feeling pretty decent; they gave you the comfort you have been seeking: "they like me," you tell yourself, "I got this!" Until that ONE student arrives. You know who I am referring to, the "one" where previous teachers told you "good luck with that (one)." The student approaches your door head low, too cool for school attitude, making his way to the very back of the classroom where he sits leaned way back with no care in the world. You being the rock star you are will make your way to greet him with your absolute biggest smile and cheerleader voice to only get a raised eyebrow and rolled eyes in return (stop, think, reflect). What is your next move? Will this one encounter and back stories on this student sum up your entire year?

I am here to tell you, every year you will have "that" student. Come to think of it… You will have a few of "those" students

DOI: 10.4324/9781003216988-50

sitting amidst your classroom. These students are nothing to fear. Previous teachers are NOT you. Do not fall into the trap of gossip and writing a child off before you even got started. The most difficult students deserve the absolute best as the valedictorian in your room. Trust me I know that the most difficult can really push your buttons and make you question why you got into this gig; however, they need you to be that backbone. They are relying on you to be the ONE. The one who puts their previous teachers to shame and help them rise to the top because you saw such a minute light burning inside of them that you ignited. I beg of you to not give up. Keep showing up. Keep smiling big and being that overly cheery person you are. Compliment them any chance you get. They need the confidence boost, I promise you.

Speaking personally and never really encountering a student I could not reach, in fact; I keep my ears perched high listening for the students spoken of above. Once I hear "that" name reoccurring around the hallways, I would run to my admin putting in a request for those students. (Surprise! I am never turned down!) But, the real surprise to me was that not every teacher shares the same mindset as me.

I have gone on for almost twelve years thinking every teacher shares the same mindset and motivation as I towards our career; but this was not the case as I was now on the other side of the table listening to teachers and admin speak of my step-child. My stepchild, who in every way possible is "that" child. I listened as they revealed academic statuses, behavior, motivational issues, etc. Being a step-parent and a teacher myself, I wasn't at all surprised by my child's demeanor and behavior they spoke of. I was flabbergasted by the lack of motivation, drive, and concern that these teachers had towards my child. It was apparent to me that they disregarded my child in every way because at this point they were frustrated and at their wits' end of what to do to make a turnaround for my child. I listened with patience and there was plenty I could have said in return, but chose to disregard the negativity bouncing around in my head like a ping pong ball. I simply stated what is the plan? What changes need to be made to complete this current year on a successful note?

This meeting with my stepchild was a reoccurring one. It personally eats me up inside to see the lack of confidence, motivation, drive, and care my stepchild has towards school. Yes, we teachers can easily sit here and make excuses for these difficult students; it's their home life, it's who they are as a person, it's their economic status, it's because they are constantly moving from school to school. All of these factors could be right on the money, but you do not have to be the puppet to the game. You are the one to break the statistics babbled on and on by every educational book out there. You are the one to stand tall and brush away every comment made previously by co-workers to immediately fire back with an incredible compliment or comment on that student. Be the one to stop the negativity and prove to everyone that love, compassion, belief, and connection go a long way. Connect to "those" students quickly and abruptly; do not wait for the moment, just rip off the band aid and make a lasting connection. You will gain the respect of that student and possibly even change their life forever. Be that ONE, be the lifeline! Now make your way to the back of the classroom, grab a chair, lean way back and talk with "that" student!

That one,

Victoria Macicek
4th Grade Math/Science
Magnolia, Texas

Give Yourself a Break

51

Dear Teacher,

Some of the most important advice that can be given to a teacher: Give yourself a break. Teachers work tirelessly and often hold themselves to very high standards. There are times when teachers just need to give themselves a break. It is not only OK to take that break, but it is BETTER for you mentally and physically to do so. Don't be so hard on yourself if you don't finish grading papers or if you have a lesson that did not turn out as stellar as you hoped. Not only are you being a good role model if you let your students know that you made a mistake or that you did not complete something as you hoped, but you are also showing them that you are human. If you model not being so hard on yourself then maybe the students will also take that attitude and be able to give themselves a break, too.

This also means take time for yourself. If you are not mentally and physically happy and healthy then you cannot be at your best for the students. They know this. They can sense and see it. Take those personal days. Take a walk during a planning period. Put yourself on a schedule for when you will work on school outside of the classroom. (Yes – we all do it. We know that working in education is not a normal job with a normal schedule. We work at all hours of the day, often seven days a week.) Give yourself a break with this. Take time to watch that TV show, read that book, go shopping or go to a sporting event or away for a weekend – whatever it is that gives you a break. And when you take that break, that means no emails, no papers, no lesson plans, no meetings, no thinking about school. You will feel refreshed and ready to tackle the next challenge.

Julie Sessions
Director of Academic Technology, Charleston, SC

DOI: 10.4324/9781003216988-51

What Is the Secret?

52

Dear Teacher,

I see you. I see you sitting there in the staff meeting hearing the administrators "shoutout" a colleague who mastered a new technological tool. I see you swimming in insecurity and feeling overwhelmed at the thought of even trying. I know the fear of inferiority and the anxiety of comparison to your peers. I see you... but I will let you in on a secret. You don't need to envy them... you are already doing everything you need to be doing to be an amazing educator. As recent as 30 years ago, students did not have their own devices. As a matter of fact, there were no computers in classrooms. There was one large computer "lab" and the teacher had to sign up to use it. Students learned to type on typewriters with correction tape. Instead of mastering the art of how to use Zoom, they were learning to speak in front of their peers for presentations, use their own voice to settle arguments with grace, and communicate with adults respectfully. When students needed assistance with an assignment, they couldn't email the text or send a message on ClassDojo but instead had to learn to ask for help. The skills we are currently trying to instill in our students: empathy, communication, flexibility, and resilience to name a few, were done in many wonderful ways long before technology was present in the classroom. How could students do such amazing things without these technological tools?

So, here is the not-so-secret secret. Fostering these skills in students has always been a product of building relationships with them and then modeling these skills. As the teacher, these are things you are *already doing* **daily**. You show students empathy when they're having a hard time at home. You model for students using sentence stems when they're struggling to come up with their own words. When something malfunctions in your lesson, you roll with the punches and keep moving without missing a beat. You think of engaging and appropriately challenging

DOI: 10.4324/9781003216988-52

lessons for your students that have multiple entry points so students can showcase their own talents. When administrators and district leaders pile more on your plate than is perceivably manageable, you model resilience by overcoming with a smile on your face.

So, there isn't really a secret. There's only a truth. The truth is this… you are already doing an amazing job. You don't need to be technologically savvy to have students that walk away from your class and use the skills you showed them to be successful adults. You already get to know them. You already let them get to know you. You love them and model what you want them to be able to do. Dear hardworking teacher, capitalize on your own strengths and talents and don't compare your skills to the skills of others. You'd never do that to your students, but you often do it to yourself. Show yourself grace and be proud of the awesome job you're already doing.

Rachel Rinker (Principal of Orchard View Elementary School)

Live—Laugh—Love 53

Dear Teacher,

We often see these signs in stores, in homes, maybe offices. But do we ever see this sign in schools? And if we do, how is it played out in classrooms? Can it, with all of the "guidelines" schools are expected to implement on a daily basis? I think so. One of my personal mottos is "find the humor in life". Laughing is essential to finding one's balance and keeping a positive attitude in any situation, not just at school. So how can you, as a teacher, "live" this sign in your classroom?

I've taught Kindergarten for 23 years. I **"live"** in a five-year-old world for 180 days each year. I live each day listening to the tales and adventures of each of my students. Some, of course, are more vocal than others. "Living" in the same classroom as a team not only helps build relationships, but it also helps to understand each student more clearly. I find their strengths and their weaknesses. I learn their likes, and dislikes. Live in the moment! And if that moment leads away from the lesson, let it. It could lead to a new discovery, a new way to approach learning, or just a better understanding of your students and how they think. Living in their world sometimes leads to laughter…

I **"laugh"** in my class every day. Whether it's with students, with my pararo, my Kindergarten team, or at myself. We laugh. As a teacher, find those students who you can laugh and joke with easily. Those whose sense of humor is similar to yours. Children as young as five love it when teachers are silly and laughing. Those students who are more reserved will be drawn to that and will naturally want to join in. This happened to me in my class. A little boy was picking up his scissors from the floor and rather than return to his seat, he chose to just lie on the floor. I took a pic to show him what he looked like. I assumed he would be upset and complete his work. He wasn't. He could not stop laughing

DOI: 10.4324/9781003216988-53

at himself. He even said "show that to my mom, she'll laugh too". I started laughing. Then the rest of the class wanted to see what was so funny and they started laughing. Then they started hugging me. We were brought together by laughter.

Hugs are a daily show of affection for younger children. For some children, that might be the only hug they get so don't deny a child the hug they need. I know it's hard when there are so many guidelines, but living in the moment, and laughing together will bring out the **"love"** we have for each other in our school family. What do you love about your school, your administration, your co-workers, the grade you teach, your students? We can all find something that answers that question. Focus on those answers and watch the enthusiasm for your job flourish.

As educators, let's all remember to LIVE in the moment, LAUGH every day, LOVE our school family.

Caroline Gaddis,
Kindergarten
Kilough Elementary School

Be There for Every Student

54

Dear Teacher,

We all got into the field of education for different reasons. Maybe for you teaching was a calling, and you dreamed about being an educator when you were little, running a class out of your basement, tree house or local playground. Maybe you were the best student in your class when you were young and have always felt successful in school. Perhaps someone saw something special in you while you were a student and told you that you would be a good teacher. For many educators, this was your career path into education. That's great!

However, there are also a few teachers, like me, who were not the best students. We were not the best athletes. We were never voted most likely to succeed, and we were never picked first for anything. No one counseled us into the field of education. But we found our way there anyway. That's great too! Because it does not matter what path you took to be called "Maestro." The important thing is that you made it, and we are now all equal; equally empowered to influence future generations of productive citizens who will impact their communities in their own unique way. We all have the opportunity to build students up or tear them down.

So please remember this: all of your students will not be valedictorians. There is only one per year. Most of the kids in your class will be more like me. We might need you to explain things to us more than once. We might need you to translate for us. We might not have the same resources or support at home as other kids. We might be distracted and cause trouble. We might not be your favorite students. Teach us anyway. Care for us anyway. Have patience and pray for us. We are the long shots,

DOI: 10.4324/9781003216988-54

the underdogs. Be the reason kids feel valued, wanted and loved. Make your classroom a place we feel safe and comfortable to fail and grow. One day you will be remembered. Students always remember the great teachers, their favorite teachers. They also remember their worst and least favorite teachers. Which will you be? Know that you will be remembered one way or the other. Will you be the good, the bad or the forgotten?

Please look out for the poor immigrant student all the way in the back of the room. He too might someday follow in your footsteps and into his own classroom and be a Maestro like you. Someday he could be the Dean of School Climate and Culture in a school in Detroit typing this letter on how to inspire teachers as he reflects on his 23 years of teaching and working in education. There will be great demands put on you by your peers, principals, society, family and by yourself. Accept and embrace those challenges, and, as they say, "Do You." Do your best and be OK with it. Sometimes it is OK to just be OK. You don't have to be the greatest teacher who ever lived to impact a child. You just have to be present. You just have to care. Be there for kids, not just in the classroom, but be there for them in the sports arenas, be there for them in auditoriums, and be involved in their lives. Be there for all of them, not just the "smartest." Be there for the underdogs too.

Maestro Ramirez
Detroit, Michigan

I Teach

55

Dear Teacher,

> I teach music…
> I teach music to students…
> I teach music to students who are identified as having
>   special needs.
> I teach music to students who are identified as having
>   special needs and spend my days trying to determine
>   the best…
> The best practice… The best music to practice…
> The best lesson I can offer them…
> The best lesson I can offer them in music to practice…
> To practice… To practice being kind.
> To practice being kind and patient…
> To practice being kind and patient, to being loud
>   and soft. To being short and long, and to being fast
>   and slow.
> To practice life skills, and soft skills, reading skills and
>   reasoning skills.
> To be the best person in any moment that they may
>   have, through my music lesson.
> But to practice.

And in it, I sometimes lose my passion for music, or rather, set it aside, because what I do is not about being a music teacher. I don't have award-winning bands here, or a Broadway show to put up. I don't have ensembles that other schools might. It is not about the tempo, or the dynamics. It has never been about the performance of music, but about the performance of life.

There are too many obstacles my students face every day.

There are personal battles they fight every day. Their ride into school, their walking down the hall, their bodies, their minds,

DOI: 10.4324/9781003216988-55

their emotions, their need to regulate, to permeate, to react, to laugh, to cry, to ask for something they know they can't do, and to want something so much that we just can't provide at that moment. Battles tredge on and on, and we work hard to overcome these battles, applauding the very small victories that feel oh so "Olympic" in stature.

But my students come here. Every day. And they leave here, every day.

Sometimes happier, sometimes in tears. Sometimes with a bag of treats for home, other times with a stickers and high-fives.

They say "goodbye," "Have a nice weekend Ms. Natalie," "I can't wait to see you next week for music," "I hope your doggies have a good walk tonight," and every now and then, "thank you" followed by a high-five elbow, or a smile bigger than their mask.

And it's on Fridays, after I see them off, after I say goodbye to them, that I close the door to my room.

Alone, as usual, I clean my desks and chairs. I wipe down my instruments from the day. I open and post my next week's lessons to various Google classrooms. I check and recheck attendance, and I finish up my administrative tasks asked of me.

I then take ten minutes to myself. And I play some music.

I practice…
I listen…
I enjoy…
Or I cry…
I dance…
I sing… I hear.

And I am grateful that I have such wonderful souls who remind me every day that my place is more than the half hour I get to spend with them. I am more than the woman who travels around with maracas and castanets, ukuleles and bean bags. I am more than just the Music Lady.

For some, if not all of my students, it is my hope that they learn, through what I teach them in music, that they can be whatever they want. They can do whatever they need.

Through music…
Through music they learn…
Through music they learn so very much…
Through music with Ms. Natalie they learn that to the
world they may be one person, but to me, they are
my world.

And next week, all of us teachers, we will practice, and try, we will perform, rehearse, cry and laugh. We might need help, we might need to change our path, we even might need to take a break. But we will have a better day, a better tomorrow and a better understanding of each other, of our students.

One more day. One more week. One more year. One more time.

Natalie Walters
Restorative Practice Specialist
North Syracuse Central school district

Are You Ok?

56

Dear Teacher,

I know our teacher life is adventurous, nonstop, loud, every emotion experienced, underappreciated, underpaid, never a dull moment, the list is endless. I didn't even mention how at any given moment of the day, we are lawyers, doctors, politicians, counselors, etc...

Guess what? That is only a few of our superhero powers. OH, yes indeed, we are the ultimate dream team of superheroes.

We got this!

Come the end of each day, say out loud, "thank you", yes, to yourself along with taking three deep breaths. Inhale that sweet smell of accomplishing the day and exhale any negative thoughts that enter your mind. Inhale the calmness of knowing that a good night's rest is coming and exhale anything you forgot to do that day. Inhale the fact that tomorrow is a brand new day and exhale any tightness in your joints. Then say to yourself, "I got this!"

Side note: if today was not your best day and you felt like screaming, well, did you?

Scream.

Go ahead, right now and scream. It's ok not to be ok at times. The problems come when you get stuck in your emotions and cannot find your way back to the "calmness".

You will find your way back because you are a teacher. We are resourceful and there are others out here like us ready to help. Be that safety net to help you get back up when you fall. Just like we do when helping one of our students. Granted, each new day will not always be your best day, but I believe in the understanding that there is something good in the day. You woke up this morning, another chance to begin again.

DOI: 10.4324/9781003216988-56

Remember... greet each new day with a smile and a grateful heart. It definitely can be a game changer on which direction your tone, your attitude, your mindset will take that day.

Well, sweet day to you.

Sincerely,

Danielle Evans, a perfectly imperfect fellow teacher encouraging you and reminding you that "you got this."

We See You

57

Dear Teacher,

We see you supporting the whole child, not *just* pushing specific academic outcomes on the child. We see you supporting the child to grow in citizenry. We see you supporting the child to *learn* social emotional skills instead of *punishing* a child when "wrong." We see you working beyond contract hours to meet the needs of your individual children because you support them as individual souls instead of individual data points.

We see you advocating for families to highlight their funds of knowledge and role as *partner* in education. We see you calling, messaging, sending notifications to families above and beyond any district expectation to celebrate your children's successes.

Teachers, we see you struggle. We see you struggle with pandemic responses, mental health for your students and potentially yourselves. We see you fight against state testing to lessen the anxiety your students are already experiencing during a worldwide pandemic. We see you go to school or self-train to teach virtually and risk your personal health.

Teachers. We see your heroic efforts. We see this across the educational community. And. We bow to you. Your efforts are enough for your children. Your efforts deserve the highest accolades.

Sincerely,

Cailin Kerch
Clinical Asst. Professor, University of Alabama

DOI: 10.4324/9781003216988-57

You Will Be Remembered 58

Dear Teacher,

No one ever said that teaching would be easy and no one ever said it would be difficult either. In a way, we are made to believe that the educational courses that we take are to "prepare" us for our own classes. Teachers are made to believe the classroom management procedures will go as planned without realizing that every plan needs to have a plan B, a plan C, and sometimes a plan D. I spent almost two decades in the classroom where I realized that what I was taught 20 years ago was quite different than reality.

As a person who was taught in a different generation than I teach, it's taken me some time to grasp the reality of changes within education, including the connection between teachers and students. We all have our own stories of successes and failures. We all have that one memorable child (for better or worse) that we shared during dinner conversations. But these are the stories that need to be shared with those who are looking to get into the teaching profession. These are the stories that truly make the teaching profession what it is.

The word "mom" resonates with every female who has borne a child or two. The word mom resonates with any female who becomes a parent whether biological or not. But I would not have expected to be called "mom" while at school, especially since, at the time, I did not have any kids. In fact, I never thought I would be called "mom" by a student that was not my own child. The first time I heard that word it definitely caught me off guard. But now, hearing the word mom come from a student is not uncommon during class.

It's not uncommon to hear a teacher being called mom or dad from an elementary student; it's cute how they want to give you a hug or sit by you because they feel safe while learning. However, when a high school student mentions the word mom

DOI: 10.4324/9781003216988-58

during class, it throws off the teacher. At least for me it did. Even more so, students *chose* to sit by me during class even when I used it as a "consequence" for not behaving.

As a white female who teaches in a diverse school, many of my students find it comforting to know that I'll be there for them. So it was no surprise when I heard my students call me mom throughout the year. While it has become a common word in my classes, there are times that students accidentally call me that and catch themselves doing it. I even heard a student say, out loud, "Did I just call my teacher mom?" and of course I responded with Yes!

At first, it was odd for a student to call me mom when I began teaching. But soon after it didn't seem weird to me at all. More and more students started calling me mom. Quite a few years later, some of the students still refer to me as mom and send me updates on their lives.

Story 1:

Katie Kate: At the age of 23, Katie still calls me mom even while living in a different state. She was a student of mine during her sophomore year in high school; she continued to have an important role in two of my clubs that I was a sponsor of in her last three years of high school. The year she graduated she gave me an Arizona University mom shirt prior to leaving for school in the fall that said, "Arizona State Mom".

Four years after graduating high school, she continues to keep in touch with me and has only referred to me as mom (and not my first or last name). Even her *real* mother refers to me as her second mom.

Since then, I've been called "mom" a number of times by my students throughout my teaching career. It's no surprise that I would hear the word "mom" many more times.

But there is more to this story of understanding and learning. It's not what students say, but it's also how they act. As a secondary educator (yes, I teach high school students), the connections are more real than one would expect.

Story 2:

In the last eight years, I have had at least one student who tells me that we are best friends. And my response every time, "we don't have Best Friend bracelets, do we?" The students laugh and the lesson continues. The next day the same student says, "good morning best friend." And again my response is, "I'm still waiting for my Best Friend bracelet."

Just as I stated before, the one student who comes in every day will say good morning best friend and each time I'll respond I don't see my best friend bracelet yet.

This went on for a few weeks. I thought I had "won" that round again until... until I walked to my desk and saw a handmade "Best" bracelet on my desk. I looked at the student and there it was around her wrist the "Friends" part. She got me. Without hesitation, I put the bracelet on and I said, "I guess we are" and class began. There was no discussion; she smiled and I smiled and that's all that needed to be done that day.

The connection I have with my students cannot be taught in the classroom nor can it be taught at a university. These types of connections are learned in the profession. Each day is a new challenge, not only with teaching but with students. There are days that students will say something so odd that there is not a response that I can think of. But there are those other days that responses come easily.

We all want to be remembered as that teacher who inspired many throughout the years of teaching. We all want to be remembered that as we take our last breath, there is that one student who is thankful for not only the learning but the connection that year.

I remember seeing a video of a group of past students surprising a choir teacher upon her retirement from the district. I remember feeling overwhelmed that seeing the joy in that teacher's face was one that I wish I could feel one day. Then I remembered my own science teacher making us feel comfortable in class while amusing himself as well as his students. I remember him doing the sign of the cross when someone sneezed. I also remember meeting my best friend of over 30 years in that class. And to this day, I remember doing the sign of the cross just as he did over 30 years ago.

Each year I wonder how or in what way I have made an impact in my students' lives and whether I will be remembered.

Kristen Koppers, M. Ed., NBCT

SEL for Teachers, Too

Dear Teacher,

Nowadays, as the world is changing more and more and as we are faced with new challenges, it has become clear that educators cannot focus on academics alone. Social emotional learning should be a priority for all students and teachers, and a major focus in every single school.

Social emotional learning is not just for kids. In order for teachers to be their best and truly take care of their students, teachers need to take care of themselves. School leaders can definitely help out with this. I think they should start by administering well-being assessments so they can identify and address the social emotional needs of teachers. After that, they can then provide support as needed in emotion regulation, mindfulness, and self-care programs. This will help decrease teacher turnover and teacher burnout, and of course, increase teacher well-being.

Once the social emotional needs of teachers are met, and they are taking care of themselves, their instruction will be strengthened, and then school leaders could implement teacher assessments in the form of classroom observations and a classroom climate survey. Once they determine the needs, they can support teachers by developing personalized social emotional learning instructional plans that may include specific programs, teaching approaches, and specialized coaching.

Of course, from my own observations, there are many teachers out there who have already been doing an amazing job providing social emotional support to their students and making beautiful meaningful connections. They are putting Doc Brad's words, "Relationships before rigor, grace before grades, patience before programs, and love before lessons," into action.

Here are a few of my favorite strategies that I believe truly make a difference:

DOI: 10.4324/9781003216988-59

- ◆ Encourage Positive Self-talk: I recently created a mirror with the words, "I am…" and all kinds of positive affirmations around it to remind my students how awesome they are just the way they are. I also included words to promote a growth mindset such as "capable," "determined," and "trying." I've seen lots of other teachers do this as well!

- ◆ Add a Daily Gratitude Routine: Every day we take the time to write down three things we are grateful for, a person who brought us joy, and our favorite part of our day. I, like many other teachers, give each child a special journal for this, but you could also just have kids take a few minutes to reflect on and share this information.

- ◆ Use Read-Alouds: Spend time as a class thinking about how the characters think and feel. Help them to see different perspectives so they can better understand people's emotions and thoughts.

- ◆ Incorporate Art: Art can be a wonderful way to target social-emotional skills. One simple example is to make paper chains. Using strips of paper, have students write a positive trait or a task to spread kindness. Then, create loops and put them together to make a long paper chain. Every day, as a class, you can take off a link to guide your SEL check in for the day. Another idea is to have kids do a partner art trade, with each one taking the time to create something special for a classmate.

- ◆ Practice Mindfulness and Provide Calming Down Strategies: Many times, kids don't really know how to calm down on their own. Teaching mindfulness can help kids learn breathing strategies, how to focus on just one thing at a time, give them go-to strategies for when they are feeling overwhelmed. I share more ideas and strategies in my book, *Educate the Heart*.

Of course, even though we know how important it is, incorporating social emotional learning into an entire school is not really something that can be done quickly or easily. I really feel that the important thing is to try, remember that practice makes better, and always keep in mind that the more opportunities we give kids to practice these important skills, the better they will be at expressing their emotions and controlling their behaviors.

Jennifer Quattrucci
M.Ed in Education Leadership and Author of *Educate the Heart*

You Make a Difference 60

Dear Teacher,

There is an old adage, "Those who can't do, teach". Those of us in education know we are so much more than just teachers. We are counselors, social workers, statisticians, teachers of social/emotional learning, kindness, etiquette, and we are relationship builders. Our job is one that does not stop when we leave the classroom. We take home the physical work of grading and planning, and the emotional work of caring. A job with such demands can never be called "just a job". It is a calling! We are called to educate future adults, fill them with the skills they will need to be successful, and to love learning so they may continue to grow in areas important to them. A lofty job indeed!

Our impact on our students may never be known to us, but we influence each and every one of them. Think back to the teachers you had in elementary school. You may not remember the content at that particular grade level but I am certain you can recall how that teacher made you (and others in the classroom) feel. You have that power to influence your students.

My journey as an educator has not been a fluid one. I taught right out of college, moved to another state, took my exams for that state, and did not teach again for 19 years. During that time away, I worked corporate jobs, had three children, and became a stay-at-home mom. I had not been in a school for over a decade before my oldest child started kindergarten. Entering her school was like coming home: the smells of glue, paper, and crayons; the sights of artwork on the walls. At that time, I was not able to return to full-time teaching, so I immersed myself in all things outside of school: PTO, chairperson for various committees, and volunteering in the classroom. When I was ready to return, the next step was to become a substitute teacher. Substitute teaching reignited my passion for the classroom. During those six years of substitute teaching, I took many professional development

DOI: 10.4324/9781003216988-60

classes offered by the district. At long last, I was offered, and accepted, a full-time teaching position.

Since those first years of teaching 19 years ago, much had changed: the amount of testing and prepping for tests, meetings and data analysis, new acronyms for everything, and social/emotional learning programs. As I reflected on the changes, there was one constant: good teaching is good teaching! For example, knowing your content well, differentiating, meeting the needs of your students, and building relationships, just to name a few.

If we are to be rid of the cliché that anyone can teach, I suggest we call ourselves educators. The term teaching is ubiquitous: a parent teaches a child how to ride a bike, a parent teaches a child how to tie their shoes. Being an educator is far more meaningful and complex than being a teacher. An educator instills knowledge in students about various subjects, and then helps them to apply that knowledge to various situations. An educator addresses the whole child by creating relationships and caring for the child. If we address ourselves as EDUCATORS, then we can be viewed with the respect we deserve, and the scope of our job can be better understood.

Yours in education,

Suzanne Trask
Educator, Colorado

Impact the Heart

61

Dear Teacher,

I work at Greeneville Middle School (GMS) in Greeneville, Tennessee. We use the Leader in Me (LIM) program to develop character and leadership in our students. I have been blessed with the most amazing group of seventh grade girls this year. Their perspective, humor, and participation has been the highlight of my school year – every single day. There have a been a handful of days that I just did not want to go to work. I was feeling tired and stressed. But remembering that I would get to deliver a lesson to these young ladies and our conversations brought the encouragement and strength I needed to not give in to myself and push on to work.

Our school started the year virtually but then changed to a hybrid platform. We had to switch back to virtual for a short time before Christmas break. Presently, we are preparing for all our students to return to a four-day-a-week format. GMS has slightly over 650 students.

I have appreciated networking with some special friends and educators in our school and system to bring food, supplies, and resources to the students on my caseload. I have a great sense of fulfillment and purpose amid all the COVID-19 pandemic and change of scheduling – virtual, hybrid, in person – knowing that I can help meet the needs of my students and their families.

Even though this year has been one of the toughest I have experienced, these girls have brought me so much happiness and joy! That is really saying a lot, too. This is my 32nd year working with special needs kids. It is only my 10th year in public school and at GMS. Previously I worked at a residential treatment facility with its own on-campus private school which served mostly special needs kids. LIM students are not assigned to me because they are sped students. I just wanted to share some things about myself with you.

DOI: 10.4324/9781003216988-61

One day in the second semester this year, the director of our school district came into my Leader in Me (LIM) group to observe. No one had alerted me in advance that he would be in the building – let alone that he would be observing in my classroom. But that is fine with me. I like to be prepared for class ahead of time and I do not put on a "dog and pony show" for anyone. Sometimes my lessons are good and sometimes they are lacking; either way, I appreciate feedback.

Later that day I saw two of my LIM students in the cafeteria at lunchtime. One of my students knew who the director was and beckoned me to her. She asked me how I was and if my day was going alright. She hugged me and told me that I had done a good job during my observation. This student is one of my most perceptive; she knew that I had been caught off guard by the director's presence. Just to keep my student feedback honest, I decided to ask another – a more flatly, less tactfully honest – student her perception of the LIM observation. My student replied that I had done "okay" during my teaching time. Then I asked her opinion as to why the director came to my room to observe. With a straight face, she replied that perhaps someone had seen me *try* to dance or do something *different* in my group and now they (whoever "they" are) are "suspicious" of me. I love my middle schoolers' perspectives!

Today, 2/21/2021, one of my LIM students' parents, who is also a teacher, tweeted the following: "My goal as we bring all students back tomorrow: I want my students to be as excited to see me as my daughter is to see @MSeaton_GMS in LIM. #impacttheheart." This has made my whole day, week, and year! (You can view/verify this on my Twitter account by clicking on my profile and then "replies" if you like.)

My students never cease to amaze me with their humor, perspective, and positivity. I know the Lord always knows what is best for us. One of His provisions for me this school year has been my LIM group. It has been my great pleasure to lead this group of wonderful young ladies!

Marty P. Seaton
Special Education Teacher

Be Courageous

62

Dear Teacher,

The work you do, the most noble and important work, reverberates beyond just the students you teach but also touches their family, their communities, their city, their nation, and the world. Your one lesson from the content you teach, your one quote you learned from someone and shared with your students, the jokes, mentorship, conversations, and projects, know that students listen, share with others, and it touches people and systems you would never imagine. All that you touch, all that you teach, you change.

As you carry out the duties and responsibilities of the teaching profession, it may seem as if they are getting longer and more difficult to manage. But don't be discouraged or dismayed. Think of the impact you are making on the world as a motivator to keep going. Prioritize what's important, which is first and foremost delivering powerful instruction for students. Everything else is secondary to that. If your school or district is not the space where you can be your best self, use your voice to demand change. As the late Frederick Douglass said, "Power concedes nothing without a demand. It never has and it never will." The future depends on you and the bold and courageous use of your voice. Remember, the needs of the teacher being met directly correlates to the needs of your students, and sometimes, the only voice they have is from their teacher. You are needed in subtle and big ways for yourself and those you impact.

Reflection truly is the best teacher and with every lesson you instruct, never leave yourself out of the picture. Center in and don't perimeter yourself out. Your personality, your stories, and your power capacity can be leveraged in a powerful way to evolve yourself and in turn evolve your students. Teach as you grow and every day as you grow, your students will be able to

DOI: 10.4324/9781003216988-62

center in with you. The best teaching relationship is when you, the teacher, and the learner, learn in exchange. Always remember to center in.

In closing, 10, 20, 30, 50, or 100 years from now, what will historians says about you? Were you complicit and compliant in the face of injustice and oppression? Or did you courageously and boldly, in the power capacity you have, do something, say something, to make the world a finer place to live. Teaching is the greatest profession in the world as all careers start from a teacher and although many don't want to respect the profession for the demanding job that it is, remember to archive your work, publicly share your work, and know you will always have at least one student who amounts to a successful career and they'll say something we teachers rarely hear, but need to hear about you and your work: Thank You.

Devin Evans
High School Teacher, Chicago

INSPIRE

63

Dear Teacher,

I have been asked to write a letter to inspire fellow teachers, so here goes.

I is for you, yourself and only you. You only have one life, maybe lots of different journeys along your way, but you need to look after you! An educator who is burnt out, cranky, tired and dreading every day in front of 25–30 students for 200 days a year is not going to fulfil the job! To help become a happy teacher who tries to see the positives in each day, you must have a work–life balance. Go for the walk, run or yoga class! Take a warm, relaxing bath and leave the marking, planning and emails until you feel you are ready to face it!

N is for no! Saying no to extra roles, duties or committees is okay! Our lives are busy enough and we don't need to burden our already overworked minds into more depths of despair!

S is for salience. Prioritise what's important and what's not! You don't need to mark every task you set your students. Your time is precious and can be used wisely by preparing lessons/resources or sending important emails!

P is for people/partner/professionals. Ask questions when you are new to the job or if you have arrived at a new school. Seek a teaching partner to bounce ideas off and ask if you can watch others teach, especially if you are new to the profession!

I is for invention. Don't reinvent the wheel! There are so many amazing websites to assist you in every way. A lot of them have free activities/worksheets and some you have to pay for but they will save you so much time!

DOI: 10.4324/9781003216988-63

R is for relationships. One of the most important things to establish in your classroom is relationships with your students! Get to know them, what they like, what they don't like, their favourite food or animal. Building connections with your students is a major stepping stone to successful behaviour management in your classroom.

E is for engagement. Engaged students are going to be keen to participate and listen in lessons. Think of different ways of delivering the curriculum in a fun way. Using concrete materials or using a game to revise a concept is always to going help engagement of students rather than teacher chalk and talk!

Shandell Gammon
Teacher in Pimpama QLD (Australia)

Find the Unexpected

64

Dear Teacher,

After teaching face to face since August 2020 and coaching a full season (33 games) of volleyball, it came as a surprise when I received an email informing me our district was going to have to go remote with synchronous learning/instruction for the first week in February 2021 due to a significant increase in COVID-19 infections within the district. We had been fortunate to have little interruption to the face-to-face learning until after Christmas break.

My heart sank thinking about the full week of synchronous learning. How was I going to inspire and motivate my high school juniors and seniors to want to log onto the Google Meet at 7:45 in the morning? In the spirit of "Where in the World is Mrs. Smith," I thought about various outside locations within my community from where I could "broadcast" my daily lessons. The locale would be the check-in question. I would post different links for the history of the location and I decided all remote broadcasts would be outside to encourage students to get outside and participate in activities that were free of charge. I would post "clues" to the location in the daily update on Google Classroom with the hope that after the first day, the students would log on before class (novel idea) to read the clues so that they could guess where Mrs. Smith would be teaching from on that day. This was the "hook" to get the students online and engaged. Afterwards, I would continue as usual with the required content and expectation for instruction and submission of daily assignments.

The first remote location was the deck of my house. My backyard bumps up to Hancock Hill and there is a plethora of paths to choose from to hike. I wanted to ease the students into this experience, be outside and, honestly, I had to test out my technology and equipment to make sure this idea was going to work.

DOI: 10.4324/9781003216988-64

I explained to my students, many times because students pretty much log on whenever they want and they NEVER turn on their cameras, about the "setup" of the week and how my remote location would change every day. The caveat to this was that to "guess" where I was, the students had to turn on their cameras so that I could see their faces.

On Tuesday, I had arranged to broadcast from the Plaine Coffee Shop which had an outside patio and was across from one of the many famous murals that are painted on buildings in downtown Alpine. I took pictures of the murals and posted before class. I also had a Google Slide with various types of coffee with the question, "Which coffee best describes you?" Once we went live, instead of 3–5 students joining with the other 12–15 kind of trickling in, I had 10 students ready to go. The excitement of guessing my location carried over to the lesson. It was a little bit like magic! I asked myself, "Could this be possible?" But, as the week progressed, each day I had more and more students ready to log on and guess where Mrs. Smith was teaching. They looked at Google classroom BEFORE class, they asked questions, they remained engaged for the regular English lesson. I was stunned. The historic Holland Hotel (it is haunted) and the famed Kokernot Stadium (from home plate, no less) were next on my list. Each day, I had more engagement from the start with 15 students immediately joining Google Meet with only 2–3 joining later. However, this was not enough. I wanted 18 students ready to engage at 7:45 am. Friday's lesson had to be memorable.

Early Friday morning (5:30 am), my clues for the remote location were on Google Classroom. I posted a video about an old desk that former students at Sul Ross University had carried up Hancock Hill, a picture of the various hiking paths for Hancock Hill, selected poems from Robert Frost, Langston Hughes and an original poem I had written. I gathered up all my courage, adjusted my hiking lamp on my head and headed up to teach my lessons from the desk on top of Hancock Hill. Because our classes start so early and we are in central time zone, I knew that once the location was revealed, I would be able to turn the computer's camera and we could all watch the sunrise together. I was scared, excited, anxious, and eager.

Once I got to the desk, I set up my equipment, turned on my hotspot and opened Google Meet. As I clicked the "join" button, I was overwhelmed because I heard the "ping" of 18 students immediately. To say I was emotional was an understatement. The kids had their cameras on, were ready to guess my location and participate in the lesson. I started to cry with excitement and one of the students said, "Mrs. Smith, it is okay, we are all here with you. Let's watch the sunrise and read some poetry." I took a deep breath, turned the computer camera and we watched the sunrise. It was a collective moment of power, deep emotion, and love for learning. Apart, and yet together we began, "Nature's first green is gold..."

This experiment with remote broadcasting is a textbook example of how the unexpected leads to a magical, teachable moment. Teachers should never stop looking for the unexpected and finding new ways to engage and motivate students.

Kristie Smith
Teacher, Clyde High School, Texas

You Can Do This!

65

Dear Teacher,

The year 2020 brought immense challenges to our profession. The COVID-19 pandemic has brought the terms remote learning, in-person learning, hybrid learning, contact tracing, quarantine, isolation, social distancing, and others into our professional lexicon. Some of you have thrived and some of you have struggled to do your job every day given the immense challenges of the pandemic. Either way, I am confident that teachers everywhere are doing the best they can. Teaching is mentally and physically exhausting. Throw in a pandemic, I am not sure what to call it short of impossible. The following hopefully serves as a reminder that what we have chosen to do is still noble, the challenges ahead are big, but not insurmountable, and leadership will be essential.

Do not forget that teaching is the profession that begins all professions. Think back to your experiences in school. Think about the classes/courses you were successful in. I bet there is a good chance that your success was related to your relationship with the teacher. My high school business teacher taught me that I was good enough to go to college when most people were counting me out. I chose to begin my undergraduate journey by studying accounting (I call it a journey because it took me seven years, four colleges, and four majors to find out I was meant to be a teacher, but that is a different story). I chose college because of my teacher. One singular person can change a student's trajectory. You have the power to determine a child's life path. Do not waste that power or take it lightly. Children are depending on you to help sort things out. This is an awesome responsibility. Teaching is still and will forever be a noble profession.

There is a common phrase being thrown around by many within the education world that is driving me crazy. It has been written and publicly stated that the pandemic has caused "learning loss". I beg of you not to subscribe to this nonsense. State learning standards, state mandated curriculum, local curriculum, state mandated assessments, etc. are ALL human constructs. The best part of these constructs is that they can be changed. They are not the laws of the universe. Fight back against the notion that students are behind. Behind what? They have experienced disrupted learning and it should be treated as such. What do we do with a student who has moved multiple times in one school year? We pare down the curriculum to the essentials and give them the interventions to be successful. Treat the disputed learning no differently. Students will be better off for it and so will you.

Teaching will always matter because of the influence we have in children's lives. I define leadership as influence. If you influence others, you are a leader. Teachers are the natural leaders of any school. Use your influence to make your colleagues better. Help other teachers get back to believing that teaching is a noble profession. Be the light that shines in a grade level, department, or faculty meeting. Influence others by being the example of what it means to be a professional educator. That is what we are. That is what you are. It is the greatest job in the world.

What we choose to do every day has impacts far beyond our current lens. I have had the opportunity to hire my former middle school students as teachers in my district. A small part of me believes that I had a hand in their success and their wanting to become a teacher. Show students that teaching is an awesome job. Show them that the teaching profession is a job that they want when they get older. You can do this!

Yours in education

Jeffrey Evener
Education Leader

Relationships First

66

Dear Teacher,

First, I just want to say that you are doing an amazing job! I see you juggling family, side businesses/second jobs, and teaching on top of dealing with a traumatic event: a global pandemic. During these trying and unprecedented times, we are working our butts off and I want to commend you for adapting to a situation none of us could have prepared for. If this pandemic has taught us one thing it's that four walls do not define us as teachers. We have accomplished so much more than we could have ever imagined virtually, in person, and in hybrid settings. We do not need a physical classroom space to educate, to learn, and to grow. We have worked so hard, persevering through the stresses and uncertainty of the last school year and this school year and we have done so with grace, patience, and flexibility.

As teachers, we are constantly going above and beyond and giving teaching our all. That is just how we are hard-wired. However, I want to remind you of an important message: don't feel guilty for letting your job just be a job. I think too often, as teachers, we go through a time in our lives during which teaching is more than a job; it consumes us. We live, sleep, and breathe it. Trust me, I have been there. But in this profession, we need to set boundaries and make time for ourselves. I would highly encourage you to find balance: treat yourself, read a book, work out, or catch up with a friend or family member. Whatever you do, try to leave schoolwork behind you on the weekend. I know this is difficult but at least take Saturday or Sunday to yourself! Here's a little secret: you can be a good teacher and still look forward to the weekend.

My biggest piece of advice is to always do what is best for the kids. Put relationships first, everything else second. Once you build relationships, everything else falls into place. Work hard to establish and maintain relationships and connect with

DOI: 10.4324/9781003216988-66

every single kid. Get to know your students, their personal lives, hobbies, strengths, weaknesses, etc. Show up to sporting events, choir/band concerts, musicals, and any other event you are invited to attend. Put their names into word problems and plan lessons around activities they enjoy. These small things seem so simple but make a world of difference. When students feel appreciated, loved, and supported in your classroom, they respect you and are more inclined to meet your expectations and try to do well. Now, of course, there are some exceptions to this. Remember, the students that need love the most will ask for it in the most unloving ways. Talk to those students, find out the root of the problem, and work with them to remedy it.

Teaching is one of the most rewarding yet challenging professions. Most days you will come home mentally, physically, and emotionally drained. The workload never ends nor does worrying about your students. But please know, you are making a difference each and every day. To teach is to touch a life forever.

Jamie Miller
7th Grade Math Teacher

Be Grateful

67

Dear Teacher,

Making a difference – being a light and source of hope and love is my calling. For me, working with children has been something I always wanted to do. From an early age, I started babysitting and serving in childcare at church. As I grew up, I said I would either be a nurse or a teacher. And when it came time, I chose to go into teaching because I saw more opportunities to use my creativity and have the most consistent impact on the children in my care.

It is interesting how God uses the challenges you go through in life to shape and equip you with tools you can use to help others. Little did I realize that the trials I went through as a child would become my "why" I teach. No one, including my teachers, knew it at the time, but the family I grew up in experienced much brokenness. Divorce. Remarriage. Moving away from family. Molestation. Manipulation. Secrecy. Heartache. Heaviness. And no one knew. Looking back, there were many times I don't know how we played family so well. It is only God's grace and the faith He gave me that got me through. Over the years, I have learned so much and experienced the beauty and freedom of forgiveness while finding the courage and strength to set boundaries.

And so, all the details left unsaid have shaped me into who I am today. Yet, it is because of what I learned in the difficulties that I now share some of the greatest contributions I have made in education. Primarily, the building of relationships. Obviously, I do not share my life story with my students. Yet, my eyes and heart are open to their needs. There are more children like me out there. I teach because I care. I want to strengthen their resilience and character and help them be successful.

When I look at the students, I see them as people who will grow up to do great things. Individuals who are born having magnificent worth and have much to offer. Students who come

DOI: 10.4324/9781003216988-67

from different backgrounds, who have a variety of needs, and whose needs change daily depending on their circumstances. I want to be a steady source of hope for them, to give them security and love... like many of the teachers I had growing up did for me. Even children who have the best of home lives still go through difficult times, and I desire to come alongside them and let them know it will be okay.

Yes, I get to teach students to read for understanding, think critically, write fluently, and use proper grammar. I encourage them to ask questions, advocate for themselves and others, and model what it looks like to be a life-long learner. I give them opportunities to practice speaking and listening skills in a safe environment where they are supported, without the fear of being laughed at when they make mistakes. I get to help them understand the importance of having a growth mindset and the value of reflecting on their learning to make improvements. They are in a protected place where we practice and develop soft skills that are essential in life. I teach them the value of taking responsibility for their actions and becoming self-directed learners. But at the heart of my instruction, the most important thing I give them is love. When they walk into my classroom, they are part of a family. And in this family, we honor one another, walk with integrity, persevere when things are hard, and communicate. My love is shown in countless ways each day through smiles, greetings, listening, making eye contact, conversations, encouragement, being available, and authenticity.

And so I write this letter to you, dear teacher, because just like the students in my care, you are a person having magnificent worth and have much to offer. You, too, face struggles of various kinds. Some are personal while others come with the ever-changing nature of our jobs. Your needs, sacrifices, and generosity do not go unnoticed. And although I may not have officially met you, I feel like I know you. You are special. You are important. You are appreciated. You are loved. You are making a difference.

In fact, your creativity, flexibility, and collaborations are pretty amazing. Working together as a team, there is no end to the things you have and can accomplish. There is an unspoken understanding between educators of all this job entails and because you know the daily joys and challenges, you take opportunities to walk alongside one another and lift each other up. You support each other by spreading kindness. Checking on the person down the hall. Celebrating birthdays, babies, and successes. Signing a card or acknowledging a loss. Bringing donuts, snacks, chocolate, or coffee for your team just because… Reaching out to the new teacher or substitute to make sure he/she is doing okay. A little empathy and kindness go a long way. And you are really good at showing it. When you get tired, you keep on. Why? Because each day counts and each person matters.

So thank you for all you do. Thank you for sharing ideas, resources, sharpies, paper, dice, books, Google slides, and everything in between with one another. Thank you for modeling patience and coming up with plan B (or C) when the internet is slow, your smartboard is not loading, and your learning platform is down. The time you spend as you gather data and fill in another spreadsheet to make sure each student's needs are being tracked and met is not taken for granted. Thank you for persevering when your planning period gets filled with yet another meeting and you are already behind with grading and responding to emails. Your diligence and work ethic is inspiring.

Thank you for coming up with scavenger hunts, Bitmoji classrooms, and creative ways to connect with your students and make virtual learning fun. You have been incredible at juggling online, hybrid, and face-to-face learning while trouble-shooting technology and learning to use new tools in real-time. Thank you for finding ways to connect students' prior knowledge with what they are learning and helping them understand how it applies to their future. What a blessing this is for them though they may not realize it at the time!

You have a great way of finding humor in situations beyond your control like when the copier is jammed and you can't find that little piece of paper stuck behind slot "D." Your desire to grow is shown when you try strategies that meet the diverse needs of your students after you learned them in a professional development session the day before.

Thank you for the grace you give to the student who has missed multiple days and is catching up on all his assignments.

You are making a powerful impression and contributing to him maintaining a positive attitude and effort towards academics. It's really not about the grades. It's about the person and the process. The grace you give reinforces this.

I could go on and on with reasons to be grateful for you and all you do. And so, the next time you feel overwhelmed or discouraged, remember how much you are appreciated. Give yourself grace and space to take a deep breath. You are not alone, overlooked, or forgotten. You are making a difference in countless lives. And even if we never officially meet in person, I am so grateful to be working alongside educators like you.

With gratitude,

Amy Bell
Teacher, Forsyth County School System

Know Your Students

68

Dear Teacher,

As I reflect on my life as a student and teacher, the most important moments in my life were those that teachers took the time to get to know me and those moments that I took to know my students. It was about listening, supporting and taking the time with students. This can be done in small moments; as students enter the classroom, a break during a lesson and as students leave the classroom:

- ◆ Movement activities (there is so much that can be done in 3–5 minutes)
- ◆ 2×10 rule (spend individual time with two students 10 minutes each day)
- ◆ Start the class or day with a quick question (favorites, weekend activities, etc.)
- ◆ Mindfulness (Mindful Moments, Mindful walking, etc.)
- ◆ Meditation (start with 3–5 minutes)
- ◆ Partner up and reflect on a question
- ◆ This or that (two pictures and students share what they like and why)
- ◆ Soft skills lessons (flexible thinking, collaborating, empathy, listening, problem solving, etc.)

This doesn't take away from the curriculum, but adds to the education of the whole child. The advantages? Greater engagement, stronger relationships and improved social skills. You will notice students' engagement goes up and they can actually learn more.

I was in second grade when I met Mrs. Criswell. She was rigorous, yet friendly. She always greeted me with a hug and a smile and spent time helping me understand what we were learning. I remember sitting with her at the table while everyone was working or had free time. I think back to those moments and

DOI: 10.4324/9781003216988-68

now understand she cared for me. She spent time with me and helped me learn what I needed to know. I know she was giving me extra support or teaching me concepts and skills new ways. We had high school volunteers in our classroom and I have one fond memory of that year. Mrs. Criswell invited me to her house to make a cake for our volunteers. We drove in her big white car to her house and I remember her being very patient with me. She let me participate in every part of making the cake from gathering the ingredients to mixing them. She supported me every step of the way, just as she did in the classroom. The next day she allowed me to carry the cake into the classroom. Needless to say, I was beaming. I remember that feeling like it was yesterday and I knew at that moment that Mrs. Criswell loved me. I know that my experiences with Mrs. Criswell had a bit to do with what she taught me and a bit of the content, skills and strategies. A unique balance in what, how and why to teach anything.

As I think about the time I spent with Mrs. Criswell I can't help but think about those things that make a great teacher. The first is understanding the power of relationships. I don't think I would have worked as hard as I did if I thought Mrs. Criswell didn't care for me. I know I went above and beyond and gained so much more from school than in other classrooms where the teacher did not know who I was, what my likes were or what my family life was. As a teacher I always extend the same to my students.

This is year 27 of teaching for me. Understanding my students and greeting them is not enough. It's important to think about what I know about them as a person. What are some of their likes and dislikes, hobbies, sports, etc.? I gather information almost daily in our conversations and activities and when I am teaching content, skills and strategies. All of our interactions are an opportunity for learning about the students we teach. In addition, there are opportunities to understand our children in school and out. We can get a sense of what their home life is like and what their needs are to be successful in school. How might we teach the whole child? You will never know the impact you can make on a life.

I know that Mrs. Criswell was the reason I became a teacher. I knew I could make a difference in the lives of the children I taught, just like Mrs. Criswell did with me.

Monica Fitzgerald
Teacher, Syracuse, NY

More Than a Teacher 69

Dear Teacher,

As an educator, you have the ability to change lives, which is what you do. There is no other profession that affects people as do educators. Without educators, there wouldn't be any other professions. But you are more than just an educator. You are a nurse, counselor, therapist, cheerleader, and most of the time, you are a surrogate parent. You have the ability to find the good in even some of the most challenging students. This year, you have come through in the toughest of times. You adapted by shifting from teaching face to face to virtual and then to a hybrid classroom in less than a year. You are the rock stars of this pandemic. You have found new ways to reach students and continue to be the solid and engaging teachers you are. And you do it all with such grace and flexibility.

If you think about what has happened to the teachers in southeast Texas, we have in one calendar year dealt with a pandemic, teaching virtually for the first time, two hurricanes, and a freeze that blacked out most of the state that caused more damage than the storms. And throughout all of this, you still kept showing up to take care of your babies. Even though you were not up to it because of what you had going on in your own home, you still showed up ready to receive your students. And through it all, you have continued to stand strong. You do it all with little recognition and little gratitude. But never forget who you are; you are the foundation of every person and every career there is. None would exist without education and teachers. You are the true heroes!

Charles D. Hawkins, M.Ed.
Administrator, Bay City I.S.D, Bay City, Texas

DOI: 10.4324/9781003216988-69

Heartwork Ambassadors 70

Dear Teacher,

Thank you for the days of delight you give to our students. Yes – OUR students – your students, my students, her students, his students, their students! The hugs, the handshakes, the help and healing and, most importantly, the heartwork you share day in and day out, month after month and year after year! You hold a special place in this world with your kind deeds, extra hours, expertise, personal resources, continuous learning, and unconditional love. You turn okay days into great ones with a wink, nod or a smile and do so with ease and confidence. You continuously send a message of hope, trust, belief, and advocacy for students when you put the needs of them at the forefront of every interaction. They feel it and know you love them even though they may reciprocate in ways that only a teacher understands and appreciates! Your students feel heard, seen, valued, respected, and honored by your actions, positivity, supportive language and never-ending devotion to their betterment. You do all of this with unwavering passion and commitment felt for a lifetime. Such an honorable profession you have chosen as part of your life's purpose!

The early mornings, late evenings, and weekends spent making life better for them may seemingly go unnoticed until the day things click. These moments are priceless, plentiful, continuous and life changing for students because you chose to invest in them tirelessly and unapologetically. Some days, months and even years may pass before you hear a thank you, but please know that your work matters and is not done in vain. The strong, fierce, funny, imperfect, and passionate teach. Don't let anyone try to convince you otherwise. You are some of the most decent, kindhearted, hardworking, loving individuals this world has to offer. You have answered a calling that most people shy away

DOI: 10.4324/9781003216988-70

from and simply could not do as well and as thoroughly as you do day after day with little fanfare and recognition.

Please continue to pour your heart, mind, and soul into your students for the rewards of doing so heal hardened hearts, open up minds and make this world a better place to be in. Thank you for always having a welcome mat at your classroom door that reads, "Heartwork Lives Here."

Kindest Regards,

Christine Delaney Bemis
Proud Public School Educator
Massachusetts, USA

You Are Not Alone

71

Dear Teacher,

Teaching in "normal" circumstances is hard. What we have gone through in the past year can truly be described as traumatic. You may often feel weary, discouraged, disconnected, exhausted, and vulnerable. I see you, I hear you, I feel you. I'm no motivational speaker or brilliant wordsmith, but I have always considered myself empathetic, and so my aim is let you know that you are not alone. So many of your colleagues around the globe are feeling the same.

Here are my hopes for you...

I hope that those around you nurture a better appreciation for each other and the importance of teamwork, support, and real recognition of the trauma you have experienced. Find people that make you feel listened to and valued. You deserve to have a voice. Don't let anyone silence you!

I hope that you continue to have deep empathy for others, while still prioritizing your own mental health. Don't cave to the pressure to appear "fine" and invalidate the emotions you are feeling. Identify and accept your emotions. Negative feelings of stress, sadness, anger, or fear are valid human emotions. Gratitude and pain can coexist.

I hope that your family/classroom connections become stronger. Many parents/caregivers think you are a rock star (don't listen to the haters!). Make connections with those families in any way you can – they will lift you up. Get creative! In our school district one of our Kindergarten teachers has parents/caregivers sign up to do read-alouds to the class through video conferencing. It's an easy way for parents/caregivers to still be involved in the classroom, and the students love it! The creativity that I have seen emerge from teachers and schools in this very challenging time is inspiring.

DOI: 10.4324/9781003216988-71

I hope that you make balance a priority in your life, and that you experience genuine moments of joy. Take breaks from social media, which can be a breeding ground for toxic positivity or just plain toxicity. Do things that make you feel content and alive. Celebrate the little victories.

There is light at the end of this long, dark tunnel. The light you emerge into may be as simple as a new perspective on some aspect of teaching, or a whole new life path you decide to travel on.

All the best,

Renee Langevin
Communication Coordinator and Technology Integration
    Specialist
Richmond, Vermont

The Power of Value

72

Dear Teacher,

A few years ago, I walked into a restaurant to have lunch. A young man brought out my food and sat down across from me. He asked if I remembered him. In fact, I did; he was a former student in my class from a few years prior who slumped in his chair, never participated, and rarely completed work. I called him by name and asked how he was doing. He said he was doing very well and wanted to thank me for what he learned in class. He told me he had listened to and acted upon every word I said about being successful in the workplace and because of what he learned in my class had recently been promoted to manager of the restaurant. This was a moment educators dream about but do not often experience.

I had been a high school band director for 17 years. I had earned my undergraduate degree and first graduate degree in music education. I was good at it, but it was time for a change. First, I ran a pilot program in conjunction with the district's virtual school franchise. I enjoyed it but there were rumors the pilot was ending. Then, shortly before the new school year began as I drove to the mountains for a quick getaway, the principal called to inform me he was assigning me a new role. I was to teach a life skills class to low-performing students. I knew the class. It was just down the hall; an "easy A" full of kids with bad reputations. They were loud. They were disruptive. I had rolled my eyes more than once at the situation. Some decisions we make, and some are made for us. However, the principal's decision changed the trajectory of my career ultimately for the better, and I became a better educator because of the work I got to do with these kids. The class, a career and technical education life skills class, was not a class I sought to teach but those four years I found deeply rewarding... a true learning and

DOI: 10.4324/9781003216988-72

growth experience (for me) that centered on helping kids find their strengths and worth within a system that valued reading and math scores above all else.

In class we focused on personal strengths and skills, careers, and pathways. We learned how to get jobs, keep jobs, and even get promoted. We learned about multiple intelligences and that intelligence could be measured by factors outside of reading and math scores. We learned basic economics, money management, and how to do taxes. At times I allowed them to be the teachers. We learned about culture, small engines, pickup trucks, and football. We learned about and celebrated their involvements and successes outside of school.

I experienced real joy as an educator watching kids' faces light up when their intelligence was praised and when I saw those who rarely found success in school enjoy learning. I loved seeing once-shy learners conquer challenging concepts and work in class. I loved hearing about the jobs they won and the raises and promotions they earned. I loved seeing their self-esteem grow. These kids were anything but low performers. I have been fortunate to see so many of "my kids" become positive contributors to the community. I believe these young people just needed to feel valued for who they were and the skills they possessed and could build, instead of being identified by their weaknesses exposed by a flawed testing system.

While teaching this class, I learned the skill of intentionally helping others see their value, and the profound effect that value (or lack of) has on self-worth. When I moved out of the classroom and into roles of supporting school staff, I carried that intentionality with me. As a band director I understood the concept of value through my knowledge and implementation of team structure and our successes, but it was easy working with high academic achievers in a co-curricular program, so I was not very intentional about it. As leaders, whether in the classroom or of the school, we can either tear people down by focusing on weaknesses and demeaning contributions, or we can build them up by giving specific praise, valuing skills, and focusing on strengths. People who feel valued hold their heads higher, are more engaged, and more motivated. And that is good for everyone, staff and students alike. Build them up.

Jody D. Alexander
Principal, Navajo Middle School

Yes, You Can!

73

Dear Teacher,

You are a teacher because you have the innate ability, desire, and passion to change someone's life and educational trajectory. You have the heart and compassion to work harder than anyone else to help a child. You share a smile with all your students to show you care.

As a Teacher, Yes, You Can!

You often think of the long days and countless hours spent on the weekend creating that perfect lesson, so your students will never forget what you taught them. You consider the alternative, but quickly realize that you chose Education in order to help children's dreams come true.

As a Teacher, Yes, You Can!

Your hard work is often not realized until much later, when students from previous classes call to let you know it was because of YOU and your inspirational spirit that they now have the career of their dreams. Because of you, they are the first in their family to graduate from high school and then college. Because of you, they are happy and living the life they only dreamed they would be living. From the student who always seemed to struggle more than most, what you hope to hear from all your students are the heartfelt words "thank you."

As a Teacher, Yes, You Can!

You unknowingly inspire the student who struggles to connect with others in the class, because you show how much you care.

DOI: 10.4324/9781003216988-73

You unknowingly make a difference for the students who feel that they have no one else supporting them as much as you. You instill hope and belief in your students that everyone can learn. You share countless words of encouragement for them to always do their very best.

As a Teacher, Yes, You Can!

You knew that changing the lives of students would be an uphill battle. Yet, here you are in the field of Education where you will continue to touch the lives of every student you teach. You are not only making a difference; YOU are the difference!

As a Teacher, Yes, You Can!

Only an educator knows the true rewards of being a teacher. Continue to fight for what you know is right for your students. Be the voice for your students and show them how to stand up and be noticed. Gratitude and appreciation may never be expressed by some, but there will be many students and their families who will be forever thankful that you chose to be a teacher.

As a Teacher, Yes, You Can!

As a teacher, you persevere! As a teacher, you are meant to do this job! As a teacher, be the one they will always remember!!

From one Educator to another, may you always be inspired!

June Tribble
Principal, Haw Creek Elementary

Informal Moments, Immeasurable Bonds

74

Dear Teacher,

As I have aged and ascended in years of experience, I became confident and more comfortable that rushing into lessons to maximize instructional time really wasn't providing more or better learning. I worked on trying to discover and find morning routines that were welcoming, engaging, simple and, most importantly, fun to build a wonderful flow and great momentum for the day. I've used scavenger hunts, crosswords, Sudoku puzzles, web exploration and chair aerobics to begin the first 10 minutes or so of every morning.

One particular activity that I recently used was to share a picture on the board. I first asked students to orally reflect on what they saw, then how they felt, followed by what they inferred and then wrapped up with creating a title for the picture. And when that 10-minute warm-up activity was done, we then went back and took the words we shared and made a five-word poem about the picture. No explicit curriculum target, no designated standards to meet, but it was an activity that allowed us to connect, interact and get us ready for the day ahead.

This type of activity for me and my class has been simple yet revolutionary. These 10 to 15-minute warm-up activities allow time for me to connect and enjoy my students' presence and slowly begin to engage and get ready for the day's activities. In the up-and-down flow of teaching, this little activity and classroom culture shift has really helped foster many more UPs and ensure better days are starting with UPs. This also allows,

DOI: 10.4324/9781003216988-74

however, for me to see where my students are every morning, so that I can get a real sense and vibe of what I need to do next.

Chey
Middle grades teacher and cohost of Staffroom Podcast

In all my years of teaching, the greatest moments have arisen from the real and vulnerable conversations that my students and I have had together. I have always fallen victim to going off on tangents with my lessons in class. Many times, we begin a lesson with a particular topic related to the subject, and through questioning and making connections to the topic, we find ourselves veering off in different directions with the conversation. I've come to truly enjoy these moments, since much of our "real life" learning happens in these informal and informative conversations.

More recently, I've begun to create these moments as a reflective process at the end of physical education classes. I've noticed that there is always a collective nervousness and excitement surrounding our fitness classes. Students have both a love and hate relationship with these exercise sessions. They are challenged by the workouts, but they have come to really appreciate the after-effects of the process. They enjoy how they feel – accomplished and exhausted in the greatest possible way.

I have always participated in the workouts alongside my class, so that they can see proper form, but also so they can see that I'm a participant in these learning opportunities, and not merely an authority figure to deliver the content. Students have always appreciated that I participate with them. I've often heard comments like, "I've never had a teacher workout with us before," or "Ms. Wander doesn't mind getting sweaty at school – that's so different." These moments have allowed us to connect on a more personal and intimate level in our spaces.

We often complete a workout and everyone is more friendly and cordial with one another. We have open and honest and FUN discussions after we collectively experience this difficult event, sometimes involving burpees, together. We overcame a tough challenge as a group, and now we can relax and enjoy the endorphins together. This post-exercise adrenaline rush also leads to many mind-clearing moments that allow for unclouded conversations that we can now use to address perhaps some challenging topics in our spaces.

I personally have really come to enjoy these talks with my students, and I know that they have also added them to the "love" section of the "love and hate" feelings they have with vigorous exercise. All in all, the relationship building has become incredible after enduring a difficult task together as a group, and I value those moments each and every time.

Pav
Middle Grades Teacher and Cohost of Staffroom Podcast

Follow Through

75

Dear Teacher,

When you hear the words follow through as a teacher it's easy at first to think to yourself, "of course I will follow through with all my duties as a teacher. I would never let my job go." So here I am – a teacher of 13 years teaching in a pandemic world wondering how to keep my head above water most of the time this year and here to tell you after treading water various times over the years that you truly do have to be intentional to make sure you can follow through with all the plans you will have each year. I can say this because I am the woman who has the best intentions ever! I am going to be the best teacher every single day, bake the tastiest treats for the workroom every Friday, have a Pinterest-worthy classroom, wear that teacher "Outfit of the Day" to turn heads, and smile while doing it all. Guess what – that's setting you up to fail because we can't do everything for everyone. What we can do is set small goals and follow through with them. When I say follow through with your commitments, I mean decide what is most important and focus on that! For example, if you decide you want to become a better math teacher this year, set a weekly goal to plan a new manipulative lesson or STEM activity and try your best to follow through with it. If you want to become more involved as a faculty member at your school, choose one committee that you know you can become passionate about and follow through with the works that will help you with becoming a more involved teacher. You can't follow through with every-thing you want to do if you overcommit. It's just not possible. Things will begin to fall through the cracks, you will blame your-self, binge eat a tub of ice cream (honestly needed at times) and overall feel like you aren't being the amazing teacher you are.

When we are intentional and set tangible goals for ourselves, it's amazing what it does for our self-esteem and overall how it gives us confidence to keep being our best teacher self. We set

DOI: 10.4324/9781003216988-75

goals every year for our students. We don't give them a goal we know we can't help them meet without the proper supports. We give them goals we know they will rock out! We want them to succeed and cheer for them when they thrive. We tell them we will help them triumph no matter what we have to do and we follow through with that until the day they leave us. We have to do that for ourselves fellow teachers! Set small goals, give yourself grace when it's overwhelming, pick yourself up when you feel like you're failing, reevaluate and keep going. Every huge change in schools, our country, your life happened because of a follow through. Just imagine what we are about to accomplish in the educational field when we continue following through with all the amazing things teachers have started together this year. You are playing a part in changing the world – just keep following through.

Mindi Mcnabb
Teacher in Tennessee

I'll Keep Going 76

Dear Teacher,

March 2020, I was not as alert as I should have been to the potential impact of the impending lockdown, predicated by Covid-19, and the devastation it would wreak on the educational landscape worldwide. During the week of the lockdown, I went about my regular business. I spearheaded a "Poem in your Pocket Day" and ran a professional development workshop for a primary school; so, I was tramping on. Then the lockdown came. Like you, I became inundated with a whirlwind of changes for which I was not prepared: We stampeded online without much preparation for new instructional practice, which carried with them the exact expectations for learning outcome assessment strategies. We were on call 24 hours a day on all kinds of social media and learning platforms. Some of us, even while we were flat on our faces, we rose to the occasion. That is something that teachers should never take for granted.

I painted the scenario above to reflect that teachers are a robust, vibrant, resilient, productive, energetic, brilliant, forward-thinking set of people. We should always find some space to be grateful for the opportunity to learn, grow and develop from all our experiences.

We have seen time and time again how our combined synergies within our various institutions have created waves by achieving things we thought impossible because of myriads of impediments – institutional, personal, professional. Though varying in degree and intensity, we remain motivated and focused. As simple as it might seem, we are blessed because we have not experienced a whole scale withering of our collective will, though pressed by hardships.

In this light, I affirm your value, each unique set of abilities, your commitment, and what they contribute to the collective mission of teaching, locally, regionally, and internationally.

DOI: 10.4324/9781003216988-76

I affirm our stance to choose hope over fear that our educational system will collapse.

I affirm your stance to push on when sitting down might have been more immediately gratifying.

I affirm each time you chose patience over frustration or even anger at the many things that go wrong daily.

I affirm each time you chose kindness.

In times of significant challenges, I encourage us to be more spontaneous with our words of praise. I encourage us to inspire confidence and courage and to rebuke fear. I ask you to embrace hope, gratitude, positive desires, love, trust, compassion, and acceptance. And, anytime we give less than we should, make a decision that would dishonour our deep-seated beliefs about why we teach, I invite you to chant this poem with me:

"I'll Keep Going." By Ann-Marie Wilmot, 2014

I'll keep going every time I fail,
I'll keep going because I must prevail.
I'll keep going when I stumble and fall,
I'll keep going when there are no signs on the wall.
Eyes are on my goals, well set,
I'll achieve them all.
I'll keep going; you've not seen the best in me yet.

I am never defeated in this life if I stick to my goals,
It's the quitter who stumbles and folds.
If I fail and becomes faint at heart after trying my best,
I'll keep going, chose another path, after a bit of rest.
Failure reminds me I am sometimes weak
  but points me to the strength I must seek.
I start; I'll finish; you bet!
Remember, you have not seen the best in me yet!

Whenever the burden of life challenges my balance,
Whenever life is bleak of chance,
Whenever my feet forget to dance,
I'll keep going.

I'll keep going in the rain or shine
I'll keep going when I'm the only one left behind, and
    my support system declines.
You see, when I kick against the prick or pebble and
    stumble
I will reject ridicule and remain humble
This is the first staging of my main act
I'm duty-bound, no turning back.

Ann-Marie Wilmot Ed.D.
Lecturer, Educational Planning and Management & Leadership,
Jamaica

Believe in the Possibilities

77

Dear Teacher,

You may have seen *Mamma Mia* and remember the great sound-track. One of the songs really stuck with me, "Take a Chance on Me". I've been teaching for almost thirty years. Each year, there's always at least one student who seems to need a little extra encouragement. Sometimes that child needs more than encouragement; they really need someone to believe in them. I've done my part over the years for many of these kids. Most have gone on to do well in school, which is wonderful!

The hard part is sometimes you don't know if what you're doing is really making a difference for this child in the long run. Last spring, when schools were shut down as the coronavirus pandemic began, I had a puzzling situation. I teach elementary gifted, so my students are with me for several years. My concern was a student who had just transferred to our school at the beginning of the year, in fourth grade. I had worked hard to build a rapport with him, since he was new. He struggled to fit in at first, but then settled in and fit well with our existing gifted class. Things were going well until March 13th, when everything shut down. I usually see my students one day per week, each grade level having a different service day. Well, the next week this student didn't show up for our Virtual Class. He didn't show up the next week either. I emailed his parents, but got no response. The third week, I emailed about the "Lunch Bunch" I was having on Friday for any of my students who wanted to hang out, chat, and eat lunch together. This student showed up for "Lunch Bunch" every week, but didn't come to class for the rest of the semester.

I struggled with how much I should say about his poor attendance, but decided to keep talking with him at "Lunch

DOI: 10.4324/9781003216988-77

Bunch" and encouraging him to log-in for class if he could. This continued for the next nine weeks until the end of the semester. He did some of the work for my class, but not all of it. Because he had done well for the majority of the year, his grades were fine. I wondered how things would be when school started again and whether he would show up.

Our next school year began with five weeks of virtual classes. This boy I had been so worried about showed up virtually for class each week. Turns out in the Spring of 2020, the family had only one device and his high school sister needed it most days for her classes. Once we came back to in-person learning, he was working harder than I ever could have imagined! He was so grateful to be in the classroom with his peers and with his teacher that he consistently exceeded both my expectations and his own. I was so excited to see his strong achievement and his progress compared to where he was when he joined our class in fourth grade.

As the semester went on, this student continued to grow in both achievement and in social-emotional skills. I was cheering him on each week! Although I was pleased with his progress, I didn't have any idea how much impact I was having on him until Christmas time. Since many students were still virtual, holiday time was different than most years. I know my students well because they're usually in my class for five to six years. Many of the kids will bring a small gift or make a card for me around holiday time and at the end of the year. This year there were fewer cards with so many students learning from home. I got one gift that surprised me. This student who worried me last Spring brought me a mug for my tea featuring Teacher Super Powers. He was so excited to see me open it, watching for my reaction. Truthfully, my eyes were a little teary. Of course I used the mug from that day forward, enjoying my tea a little bit more.

Three months later, he's still engaged, motivated, and high achieving. You never know how much believing in what's possible can impact a student!

Karen Kraeger, Ed.D.
Gifted Specialist

Don't Lose Your Joy

78

Dear Teacher,

Did you know that employees who laugh frequently and make others laugh frequently are on average four times more successful than those who don't? Don't ask me where I got that statistic. I'm sure it's true though. Not that laughter should be a means to an end... After all, wellbeing is the ultimate end goal, right? After this year of navigating educating our country's youth in the midst of a global pandemic, it's that much clearer that our individual and collective wellbeing *should* be the ultimate purpose of schools.

Sometimes, though, we get so caught up in the to-dos—in the *work*—that we forget the ultimate reason why we are doing the work.

A few weeks ago, like many of you, I reached a crescendo of overwhelm from all of this, and I did what I typically do when I'm feeling like my life is out of control: I got on my hands and knees and cleaned the bathrooms until the smell of bleach drove my family outdoors; I had a few glasses of wine and marched upstairs with dull kitchen scissors and cut off all of my hair; I bought a pond vacuum I don't need and don't know how to use because the look of the algae irritated me every time I crossed the driveway to my new home office to head to "work" in my sweatpants.

And then yesterday it hit me; my grasps for control were not combatting my overwhelm in the way they normally would because my frustration right now is less about the loss of control in my work and more about the loss of *joy*. Everything has become about the mandates we need to meet, the guidance we need to follow, the events we need to pull off, the tech we need to learn. Those things existed in the physical building too, but when they started wearing on me, I'd walk down the hall and

DOI: 10.4324/9781003216988-78

find a friend to joke around with. I'd chat to a student during tardy duty. I'd slide into a classroom where the excitement of the teaching and learning was infectious and inspiring.

My challenge to you this week is to cultivate joy. That was our mission as a school community this year. The first day of school feels like ages ago, but that was … that IS … our mission. And, in the spirit of going from great to groundbreaking, let's be the school whose laughter is louder than our uncertainty.

This has been a time of crisis indeed. But I got it wrong, and I'd like a do-over. Crisis doesn't mean putting our joy on hold until things get back to normal. A time of crisis is the exact time to fight for joy. We can do hard things. We owe it to our students to model doing hard things. Finding our joy right now might be one of the bravest and hardest things we do. It will also be one of the most important.

If hope is a better predictor of success than test scores and those who laugh are more successful than those who don't, then this week, do something silly. Do something fun. Do something in which the only purpose is to cultivate joy … and know that purpose is good enough. In fact, it is the ultimate end goal. Don't worry so much about the mandates and guidelines for distance learning as much as you worry about the last time you and your students smiled and laughed together.

Amy Fast, Ed.D.
Assistant Principal and Author

Be Vulnerable

79

Dear Teacher,

I can't spell. No, seriously. I can't spell. When I was in 7th grade, I entered the only ever spelling bee in my life; I was out in the second round because of "marvelous." I don't remember how I spelled it, but it was so wrong the announcer had to stifle a giggle before telling me I was out. Not only was I so embarrassed I wanted to melt through the floor, I had to sit there for the next hour and a half through the rest of it. Needless to say, several decades later, that single memory has haunted me. So has my inability to spell, especially under pressure.

Over the last twenty-one years I have started every first day, every class period with the same disclaimer: "I can't spell. I mix up letters and forget whole words, especially when I am trying to write on the board and talk at the same time. Please, when you see something misspelled, let me know and I will fix it. All I ask is that you be nice about it. You guys are my spellcheck." They look at me with the side-eye like, "how can you possibly be an English teacher and not know how to spell?" Inevitably by the end of the first week, they completely understand why I told them that. They also begin to let me know when things are spelled wrong, awkwardly at first, and help me correct them, even if they must google it.

Often our students are just like that embarrassed 7th grader who couldn't spell "marvelous" but are too afraid to show us who they really are. Half the time, they just need a place where they can make mistakes and not be ridiculed or expected to be perfect. Be that place. Brené Brown says that through vulnerability we can cultivate meaningful relationships. We model how to write, how to take notes, how to edit and revise; why not model how to be our authentic selves, flaws and all, and how to respect those flaws in each other? Being vulnerable is not telling others all the

DOI: 10.4324/9781003216988-79

gory details of our lives. It's being real. It's providing the space to make mistakes, be flawed, and work it all out without fear.

Teaching can be hard and every day, every class period, can feel like you are taking a giant leap of faith. Take it. Both feet. All in. All great achievement comes from epic failure. Take it from a veteran, I have failed epically and often. There were times when I thought, "this is it. I'm going to be fired" because my students tend to drive the conversations, which turn into projects, which turn into creative lesson planning and standards bending. Even then the results were worth the risk when students see the beauty in their own work and sometimes even make life-changing decisions because you allowed them an opportunity to be themselves, think for themselves, and speak for themselves. That is the magic of teaching.

One of the hardest aspects of remote teaching and learning has been the isolation. Many students who hate school didn't realize that what they hated was schoolwork, not school. They hated the confinement and lack of choices. What they miss is sitting in your class telling you how to spell what you just butchered on the board and knowing that you appreciate their help. They miss having conversations in class about what they assume is some off-topic screed that you have carefully crafted into a thematic discussion. They miss just being with people. They miss just being with you.

I imagine you miss all of that too. We don't miss the mindless meetings and pointless paperwork, or the ridiculously over-formatted lesson plans that have to be color coded. We don't miss the truly bad coffee that someone left burning in the pot because heaven forbid they start a new one (you know who you are). But we miss the little conversations about students' lives, the look on their faces when they "get it" after twenty-three tries, and the triumph when they conquer what seemed impossible to them and come out the other side as better people. We even miss them pointing out our spelling flaws on the board in front of everyone and helping us make the corrections.

When this is all over and we are back in classrooms full of chatting students, remember that students need to be seen and feel heard in order to thrive. They must be a part of something, a member of a tribe, to believe they can achieve. They need someone who will be there, who is not afraid to show them who they are, flaws and all, bad spelling, tired, cranky, and showing up anyway because it matters. They matter to you, and you matter to them. They will need a place to work through their frustrations, their concerns, their fears, and not feel judged. They need you because you get them, you see them, they are not invisible in your presence. Perhaps there will be times when they show you the worst of themselves, but that's because they know you won't hate them for it. Those days will be ugly, and you may feel helpless in those moments. Hold on until their storms pass and they will know you care enough to let them rage without turning your back on them. They will know that they are seen, they are heard, and they are enough.

There are thousands of techniques and practices I could recommend using with your students. I could talk sound pedagogy for hours, if not days. None of that matters if students do not feel safe or valued, seen or heard. If you do only that, model authenticity and acceptance, provide a safe place for them to really be themselves flaws and all; the rest will happen on its own. In return, your students will confirm that you are also valued, seen, and heard. You are also enough.

With love,

Dottie DePalma
English Teacher, Teacher Leader

Connections First

80

Dear Teacher,

I was speaking with a colleague the other day, and we discussed how the teaching profession is like a marathon and not a sprint. At the beginning of our careers, we see endless possibilities and want to try everything. By the middle, we are often worn out from endless initiatives, greater expectations piled upon our overflowing plates, and a lack of support to accomplish it all. Sometimes, it can feel as though we are crawling ever so slowly over the finish line at the end. But if we keep our focus on one thing, the thing that inspired us to go into teaching in the first place, we can keep pace throughout our careers and retire with gratitude, joy, and fulfillment. Have you guessed what that is?

After 24 years of teaching in Ontario, Canada, I have found that what keeps me grounded in this profession is my focus on making a difference in kids' lives. As I think back over my career to this point, I am amazed at how much the job has changed over the past two and a half decades. Teachers are expected to do more with less. We are teaching heavy curricula, facing a mental health crisis in our children, and are at the mercy of the political whims of the day. However, at the heart of everything we do is the kids we are blessed to work with each and every day.

I have learned that the key to making a difference is to start by making connections with our kids. Building strong relationships with our students is so important in the work we do. I make this my number one priority at the beginning of each school year. Kids are amazing people who crave human connection. As colleagues walk by my classroom, they will often find me sitting with a table group during a nutrition break, talking and laughing about silly jokes, our families, or our dreams. They will also see me on the floor with my students playing a board game, building with Legos, or working on a mural. Sometimes, they will even discover me at the heart of dance party following a GoNoodle

DOI: 10.4324/9781003216988-80

video! These informal, unstructured moments in the school day are where true relationships develop and deeper connections are made. The hard work of teaching becomes so much easier when I have nurtured these important relationships. Each day I strive to demonstrate to my students that I genuinely *like* them, enjoy *being* with them, and am *here* for them. When I focus on that, the rest becomes background noise.

So, seize the opportunities to just *"be"* with your students. Connect with them on a human level, get to know them and let them get to know you. When you put that at the centre, it is amazing what you can accomplish, where you can lead them, and how you can make a profound difference in their lives. This is what will carry you through the marathon of your teaching career.

Sincerely,

Jennifer Sims Murray, Teacher
Vice President
Elementary Teachers' Federation of Ontario, Niagara Local

Don't Be Afraid to Leap! 81

Dear Teacher,

Don't be afraid to trust the doors that open, even if the opportunity looks different than you planned.

I am currently an Assistant Principal at a high school just outside of Nashville, TN. The truth is, I never (a word we shouldn't use) thought I'd be in this position, specifically at a high school, but I took a leap of faith and landed where I was meant to be.

My background is in Elementary Education, certified to teach K-6. I avoided anything above 3rd grade while doing practicums in college, so of course my first Student Teaching placement was in a middle school with 6th graders. It took one week, and I realized how much I loved teaching this age group. I think my hesitation was from my own middle school experience, but I should have always been using that as motivation to make it better for others, which continues to be my motivation in how I lead today. Thankfully, I trusted that I was placed in a middle school setting for a reason and when the opportunity presented itself for me to take a position teaching 6th grade math, I made the leap.

I spent the next seven years in the same school teaching 6th grade math and loved almost every minute of it. I could write an entire book on how hard the first year was, but also how those lessons pushed me to be a better educator for it. From 2008–2015, I pushed myself to improve in relationships, classroom management, and instructional strategies. Those first two are the foundation for building a successful school. I also realized how much I loved the community of students and the impact they had on me.

In my seventh year I was finishing up my master's degree in administration and began feeling that I needed some type

DOI: 10.4324/9781003216988-81

of change. I wasn't sure what I was looking for at the time, but I knew I wanted a new challenge. A few weeks later I received a phone call from the administration at the high school that my middle school students were zoned for. Keep in mind I was K-6 certified, originally never thought I'd ever teach 6th grade, and the thought of high school never crossed my mind. A new position was being created for a full-time Math Interventionist at the high school. I was offered the opportunity to start the RTI (Response to Intervention) program in a high school setting. This completely scared me for several reasons. First, high school was so outside of my comfort zone. Second, I spent the last seven years teaching math standards; was I even qualified to teach the basic skills to 9th graders? I spent the next 24 hours putting a lot of thought into this and reflecting on my journey up to this point. In college I was an aspiring kindergarten teacher who fell in love with teaching middle school. I loved teaching math, and I loved my kids. Knowing these two things, and that I made the leap of faith once before, helped me decide that this was the next step in my journey. I found my new challenge while getting to follow "my kids" to high school.

I spent the following two years increasing my capacity as an instructional leader and learning as much as I could about administration in my role as Dean of Students. At the end of my second year at the high school one of our Assistant Principal positions was opening for the following school year. The encouragement I received and the fact that our principal considered me to be qualified to do this was the push I needed to consider applying. So once again, I found myself being presented with a new opportunity I could have never planned for. I reflected, I prayed, and then I made the leap. I'm about to wrap up my fourth year as an AP at a high school and my 13th year as an educator. I've grown as a leader, as an advocate for students and teachers, and I'm continuing to learn who I am and what I aspire to be so that I can continue to make a difference. I am thankful for taking chances, especially those that scared me. Whatever it is you're currently facing, remember that "great things never come from comfort zones". Trust that you are capable, find your support system, and make the leap.

Hayley Richardson
Assistant Principal in Tennessee

Remember Your Why 82

Dear Teacher,

There will be days you will feel like quitting. There will be days when it all feels like too much and you'll wonder why you are doing it and there will be days when nothing goes your way.

And then one day there will be a student that finally understands that word/sentence/structure you've been working on for the last few weeks/months; there will be that one student that finally can say a full sentence without help, and with perfect pronunciation. Their eyes will light up at their progress; and in that moment you will remember why you are doing what you are doing. Why you became a teacher in the first place.

Every day you get to be a light in someone else's life, a safe space for children to explore and learn new things, an Aha! moment here and there when they can finally understand, and in that moment you will know it is all worth it. You will know why you are a teacher, and you will remember why you wanted to be one in the first place.

The most important thing is that they know you are there to care for them and to nurture their learning; you are creating a lifelong learner and may even be that one teacher they will never forget because you had such an outstanding effect on their life.

I never dreamed of becoming a teacher; it was put on my path and I fell in love with teaching, for all the reasons mentioned above. Good luck out there teachers, and remember every day is an adventure and we learn just as much (if not more) from our students than they learn from us!

Husnia Lee Jakarta
Teacher in Indonesia

DOI: 10.4324/9781003216988-82

Dear Superhero

83

Dear Teacher,

To play off of the words of the late great poet, Christopher Wallace,

> *"Who the heck is this calling me at 5:46 in the morning? Crack of dawn and now I'm yawning. Wipe the coal out my eyes. See who's this calling me, and why."*

I will assume you have had an experience similar to this within the past year, only for you to eventually realize that it is in fact that dreaded 5:30 am alarm you set to wake up to on a Friday morning. Your alarm sounds off. You make the bold and difficult decision to press the "off" button instead of repetitively pressing "Snooze" every nine minutes. You shower, start a pot of coffee, brush your teeth, and get dressed all while simultaneously managing to get a toddler ready.

You, then, drive 20 minutes across town to drop that toddler off to an overpriced daycare before you speed back to an empty school building. You walk into your empty classroom and log into your outdated computer that inconveniently decides to install security updates minutes before your work day officially starts. You double check your webcam, lesson plans, and supplies before you hit that dreaded "Start Meeting" button on Zoom. For the next 7.5 hours, you are a Zoom or Google Meet teaching machine!

For a lot of us, this has been our lives since "the day the world stopped" in 2020. We are certainly dealing with uncharted waters here in the field of education. But, hey! Let me tell ya something... you are rocking it! In our field, we are always rolling with the punches to adapt to new guidelines, best practices, and even new personalities within the classroom itself. This year

DOI: 10.4324/9781003216988-83

is no different other than the punch being delivered in a Mike Tyson fashion.

You are a superhero that often goes unheralded outside of the one week at the end of every school year. Your new superpowers include: expert lesson facilitation via virtual meeting rooms, superhuman endurance when the coffee runs out, supersonic typing speed to answer questions via chat, and advanced time manipulation skills because there is no way you have enough hours in the day. All of that is in addition to the superhuman abilities you already possessed within a normal school year.

So to all of the superhumanteachercoachmomdadauntuncle grandparents out there, Thank You.

Your Brother in Arms,

Coach Rich
Lafayette High School
Lafayette, Louisiana

This is HEART-WORK

84

Dear Teacher,

I want to first thank you for your service, sacrifice and seldom acknowledged success. I want you to know that even though you are often times made to feel undervalued (you are valued), overworked (you don't have to earn rest, it is due) and overwhelmed (unclench your jaw, exhale, scream, cry, laugh, shout… walk away, but come back), you are NEEDED! This is not a job, career or profession! It is "HEART-WORK." And, with that choice, you may need a few reminders, warnings and encouragement along the way.

Hard work is different from heart work. Which is why I will never call this choice (because you do have a choice), a job—THIS IS HEART WORK! You heart is where you store and revisit your WHY. Your heart is where both your weaknesses and strengths reside. Your heart is where your thoughts, efforts, triumphs, failures and growth take seed, root, sprout and grow. You MUST guard it! Never allow a standard, scholar, student, parent, assessment, evaluation, observation or school to stop you from doing the work. Keep your eyes focused on the impact. Stick to your values, keep your intercity and wits about you. Don't allow yourself to take detours that lead to darkness or defeat. You were made for this. You have the heart for this… so make it work.

Trigger Warning!

I also want you to know that with the HEART-WORK, there comes a few occupational hazards. Like being on the receiving end of a parent's few choice words, toxic school culture, unsupportive administration or "that kid." However, the worse of them all can be "Imposter Syndrome." Imposter Syndrome will make you sit with feedback, and pick yourself apart, or cause you to replay an

DOI: 10.4324/9781003216988-84

observation in your head until you've convinced yourself your scholars are on their way into illiteracy and disnumberia. Trust me, that is NOT the case. You must condition yourself to focus on the feedback that correlates with scholar impact. If it doesn't positively or negatively impact your scholars or your promising practices, table it. Ask yourself can you implement the feedback now or later. Oftentimes we make suggestions like the Bible. This becomes an unnecessary burden, so don't, if you can't. And, if all else fails, "DON'T ENGAGE." Acknowledge receipt and place it in a file for another day. Speaking of which, you have to create BOUNDARIES.

I FEEL YOU

In closing, I want you to know that your voice matters. Please never hesitate to bring voice to the positive, negative, concerns or use it to seek clarification. Just as you advocate for your students and the community you serve, you must advocate for yourself. Use your voice and platform to seek opportunities for activism, and rest, growth and reflection.

DO NOT allow yourself to be shaken by the waves of the journey because calm seas have been said to make for poor sailors. Just as quiet classrooms make for missed opportunities of discourse or informal data.

Understand that the system that is public, private or charter education is a system that is not designed for equality. We are still very much on our way to that. But, in the meantime operate, strive and fight to work from a place of transparency, account-ability and activism.

The classroom... that student... that team... that school... that district... the educational system... the world needs you. And your ripple... your impact is felt!

TaiQuay Bogle
5th Grade ELA, Florida

Educational Gardener

85

Dear Teacher,

Thank you. Whether you have heard this in abundance, or don't hear it enough: You are appreciated and valued by many; by every mind whose ideas you have helped foster, every path that has crossed with yours, every student that you have taught. Whether those interactions were brief or lengthy, they have a lasting effect. You are the gardener of intellectual seedlings that sprout daily with curiosity and grow with academic confidence. It is dedicated teachers like you that make our educational world go round. From celebrating those "ah-ha!" moments, to repressing hot tears during a busy middle-of-an-interrupted-lesson, haven't-had-a-break type of day, you remain undefeated.

I was drawn to education after experiencing first hand what a teacher with a big heart can do. I fell in love with education and the impression it has on our youth, more specifically the lasting impression it has had on someone like me. My family and I moved to a small town across the country when I was in the second grade. From California to North Carolina. I was shy, quiet, afraid, and cried almost every day. Quite the opposite of my true self. I had left all of my friends behind. Everything I knew. My new teacher was patient, kind, and outgoing. I don't remember how pretty her labels were, nor how organized her classroom was. I couldn't tell you how artsy the decorations were either, or what rules we may have had at the time. I do, however, remember her positive perspective. I remember when she would take the time to ask us before our small group how we were and if we had eaten.

Every morning she showed up and took interest in how we felt and genuinely cared about our interactions with one another, ensuring that they were positive ones. I remember that she remembered my favorite color, and always gave us our favorite color erasers. Not as prizes, but just because, "in case you need

DOI: 10.4324/9781003216988-85

it," she would say. I remember how she always gave everyone a chance to answer in the classroom regardless of how farfetched the response could be, how excited she would get when sharing a new book with us, how she was invested in our learning because she celebrated the individual skills we had, and most importantly I remember that she had feelings too. She was genuine and determined. She cared. From the very first day that I walked into that new school, new classroom, and was greeted by her with a sincere smile, she made her lasting impression on me. She was happy to see us. Something so simple that she did every morning. I share this with you because what you do every day, from showing up to work with a smile, despite what you may be going through, to greeting your students every morning even if you don't receive a response back, to taking the time to help a child tie his or her shoe, even when it's perhaps the 20th time that day, to asking them how they are and taking a moment to listen to a story, all to writing a simple smiley face and some feedback on their papers: matters.

You are a daily inspiration to your students. What do you think that they will remember about you? My journey as an educator was inspired by someone like you. Someone who shows up, someone who gives their all, someone who waters and celebrates the new sprouts. An undaunted individual. You are making an incredible difference in the lives of many. From one educational "gardener" to another, keep watering.

Rosie M. Reynosa, M.Ed.
Asheboro City Schools, North Carolina

Anyway

86

Dear Teacher,

As a school principal, it was imperative to me that our school adopt a school-wide priority each year. The priority was essentially a goal inspired by data, needs, and stakeholder feedback. But rather than writing out one more convoluted objective in a plan that was never fully known or understood, we focused on developing a simple mantra to live out for the year. My favorite priority was adopted at Albertville High School in 2018.

Most have read Mother Theresa's wise words suggesting we forgive anyway, be kind anyway, succeed anyway, create anyway, and give our best anyway. Some have probably passionately sung along with Martina McBride while listening to her song titled "Anyway." (If you have not, I highly suggest it!) But when you take this "anyway" notion and apply it in a school, in the school's main office, in the hallway, or in your classroom – the impact is incredible and you become the best version of you!

Teaching is a hard, emotionally exhausting, and often unappreciated profession. But yet, you are reading this as a dedicated teacher seeking inspiration to be the best teacher you can be. Why? I dare say because there are times when teaching is a fun, difference-making, and often rewarding profession. You know that when you take away all the mandates, complaints, political agendas, and pointless paperwork, teaching matters!

The truth is, we know, as educators, that we chase dreams that seem out of reach, but we dream them anyway. Our world has gone wild and it is hard to believe that the future will be better, but we believe it anyway. You can pour your heart into a lesson that tomorrow the students will forget you ever taught, but you teach it anyway. Sometimes things do not turn out like we think they should and sometimes we do not like what is asked of us, but we do it anyway. We do it anyway because we know that we can make a difference in the lives of our students.

DOI: 10.4324/9781003216988-86

If you adopt this mantra and live with an "anyway attitude," you will absolutely make a difference in the lives of students. If you create a safe and supportive environment for students, they will grow. If you demonstrate respect and are positive about teaching, your students will be more respectful and positive about learning. If you model fairness, your students will (one day) appreciate you for it. Your kind, honest, and compassionate words will make a positive impact.

It is so easy to slip into the negativity, to feel entitled or bitter, and to become apathetic about the work we do. I know. I have been there. But when we do this, not only do we damage our own personal lives – we cast a shadow on our students' experiences and our profession. So, I challenge you: the next time you feel discouraged, underappreciated, or burned out, remember how important you are and be the best educator you can be... anyway!

Thank you for what you do each and every day!

Deidra Tidwell, Ed.D.
Albertville City Schools
Albertville, Alabama

This is a job. FULL. STOP. 87

Dear Teacher,

When I say full, I want you to read yourself as "full," and when I say "stop" I want you to read it like a command.

This job will fill you and fulfill you, but what it fills you with each day may be difficult to stomach. Forgive me, I'm a Language Arts teacher so I am a sucker for a good metaphor. Some days you will be full to the brim with anxiety, with your students' fears and frustrations, with your own exhaustion. Other days you may feel so full of empty space that it is difficult to breathe—like the life force has been sucked out of you and all you have left is painful air.

Then there are the days of fulfillment. Those days will sustain you and they are coming. They are enough. They help.

But they don't always come when they need to.

Listen to me.

It is important to take a break so you don't quit. This is true for athletic training, studying, and it is DEFINITELY true for teaching.

On the days when you come home full but not fulfilled, I want you to remember.

"This is a job. Full? Stop."

As teachers, we want to martyr ourselves to the bone. Bones don't teach kids. People do. And you need to be a full person to teach kids. If you are full—full of empty, full of exhaustion, full of despair, full of anxiety

Stop.

Take a day. Take a day off on a Wednesday because subs are easier to get on Wednesdays. Give the kids an in-class amnesty day to complete any work they are missing (because kids are usually full by the time you are).

There are only two rules to your full stop.

DOI: 10.4324/9781003216988-87

1. You are only allowed to check email once (or if you're at the expert level, not at all).
2. No grading. No planning. Nope. Full. STOP.

I know it is easy to get suckered into the narrative of "It's too much work to take the day off. I'm going to have to do twice the work when I get back just to make up for it." You're probably right. That's okay and worth it. Athletes must increase their training when they have been side-lined due to injury. Know what happens to athletes who attempt to play through?

Career-ending errors and injuries.

When your heart is full of anxiety and fear and stress there isn't room for fulfilment. I should know. I quit in my 4ᵗʰ year of teaching. I took my toys and stomped my foot and went home. I made a good amount of money in the private sector as an insurance agent. I educated people over the age of 65 about their Medicare supplement options. But my heart wasn't in it. I needed to be fulfilled. I wish now I had taken more breaks so I did not need to quit.

I'm back teaching now. I'm fulfilled and largely because I seek joy in my days in my classroom. On dark days when I am full but not fulfilled. I stop. I FULL STOP.

Take your days off, even if it means you don't get paid that day. Take the day and do not do anything having to do with school. That way, when you come back you can seek fulfilment and not feel overly full of all of the other stuff.

I'm proud of you for joining us. Be well.

Jordan Kohanim
English Teacher, Roswell, GA

"CCR" – Culture, Curriculum, and Relationships!

Dear Teacher,

In 13 years of teaching and coaching, I can narrow "teaching" down to three key things that bring "successful learning" to a classroom or on the court or field in athletics that I have found were key to managing a successful classroom. And that is "culture, curriculum, and relationships"! Or what I call "CCR" (with all due respect to the great classic rock band of the same name!). If I was to pass along to teachers three key things to focus on to help with classroom success, these three fundamentals have been the common denominator for me in the classroom and on the volleyball court.

The first one, which could be perhaps the most important, is "culture." A positive thriving culture is so fundamentally key to the success of a classroom or athletic team that without it, everything else and all the other details in the classroom or on the court falls apart! If possible, always land at a school where "culture" is the most important thing and everything revolves around their successful culture! So much so that every decision that is made is made with the overall school "culture" in mind! That means "kids want to be there"… "teachers want to be there"… and "admin wants to be there"! And there is a sense of "pride" so dominant you would swear it is in the air!

If your school doesn't have it or you find yourself in a poor culture, then take the lead and establish your own "classroom positive culture"! If there is one thing you can control as a teacher, it is what happens within the four walls within your classroom regardless of any "school negativity" that is happening outside of

DOI: 10.4324/9781003216988-88

it! So be your "own leader" on this! Make your classroom a place kids look forward to coming to every day! This means every day they are there, they achieve some sort of success, they celebrate being around their other classmates, and they take pride in being a member of the student populous. You will find that it makes the days much more manageable when you invigorate a thriving culture within your classroom regardless of what you have to deal with outside your classroom!

The second is "curriculum"! As in how you deliver it and making sure you are staying on your curriculum! What is the common denominator as a teacher and coach I have observed over the years? Fun! The feedback I get from students is how much they enjoyed learning in my classrooms whether it was Physics, Calculus, Algebra 1, or any of the other math I have taught! I get the same response from the Volleyball court. Kids tell me they have learned so much about the game that it was the most fun they had! (and usually resulted in wins!). Kids do want to learn! They may not show it or admit it, but they do. More importantly, when they succeed in learning something, they take tremendous "pride" in that and that is everything in education. So my advice? Stay on your curriculum! And avoid using your classroom as too much of a place that strays off topic and becomes too much of a "social gathering." They have other places for that.

The other part of the curriculum equation is "relevance." As in how does your curriculum relate to the real world kids are either experiencing or about to experience? When I first got into teaching (and I didn't get into teaching until I was in my 40s), I originally thought no kid would want to hear about my experiences in the real world related to mathematics, physics, and geoscience (my background). I was totally wrong! When I was teaching physics topics related to aerial photography and satellite imaging, I shared my experiences with them all while tying it to curriculum. Kids soaked it in! So much so that when I talked, eyes were glued and the class was totally silent listening. I came to the conclusion that "kids crave relevance"! They get the school formats. What they crave is that "relevance" that gives them an understanding of "why" they are in your classroom and in your subject! So when coming up with your units within your curriculum, think about any relevant things you can use while delivering your content! You will find that it captures your classroom audience!

And finally… "Relationships"! You will see this talked a lot in the education community and rightfully so. The trick? Finding the "right relationship" dynamics with each kid. This is more challenging than it would appear because a "one approach fits all" to relationship building with students does not necessarily work for all of your students. I prefer to also use the word "mentoring" when it comes to the relationship building with my students and athletes. And "mentoring dynamics" for one kid will be different than others.

Case in point. I can have two students in my class. One is more socially dynamic and my mentoring approach to them would revolve things like "giving them a friendly greeting every day," asking them how they are doing in their extracurricular (FFA, Band, etc.), "did they see a latest movie release", etc. Why? This student looks forward to that type of conversation from all their teachers (most teachers show this kind of relationship with some students). The other student is the type that I might have some discipline issues with in my class and while they do behave, they do have days where they ignore rules. From there, my relationship or mentoring approach involves "structure" things. And talking through problems and discussing "rule following" things. And yes, at times administering consequences but at the same time, "explaining why there are consequences." If there is a day he or she accomplishes something, we celebrate and also talk about that. Why? You can't just point out corrective things without telling a student what they also do right! Most students of this type I have wound up having a profound respect for me even though there were days I have to "get on them to do the right things." Because as most said, they told me "I cared and were looking out for them!

So when it comes to "relationship building" in your classroom, please think of the word "mentoring" when you are developing relationships with your kids. Since each student is "unique" in their own way, each will need their own mentoring method. So apply a method that suits the student and makes them comfortable in your class and with you as a teacher or coach! Don't apply generic relationship building things to everyone!

So go apply "CCR"! Peace and cheers to all the educators and coaches out there! My sincere thanks to Dr. Brad Johnson for allowing me to contribute to his latest authoring venture! One of the greatest educators out there in this world!

Terry Lambert
Physics and Math Teacher / Head Volleyball Coach, Texas

You Have the Power   89

Dear Teacher,

Many young kids dream of being professional athletes, movie stars, models, famous YouTubers or even TikTok stars. As a little girl, I dreamed of being a teacher. I played school at home with a chalkboard and chalk my parents bought me and my brother had the fortunate (some may say unfortunate task) of being my student. I collected extra copies of worksheets from my teachers and big activity books from K-Mart and I was able to provide many educational opportunities for my brother (haha!). I stayed after school and graded papers with my teacher. Sometimes, I would even go to my teacher's house to help her grade papers. I always tried to be the student that I would want in my classroom.

After 25 years of teaching, every day I still get to live out that dream. I tell my students this story at the beginning of every year. I tell them: "When you don't know something, I get to live out my dream. When you have a life problem or peer issue, I get to live out my dream. When you are experiencing something for the first time and you're struggling, I get to live out my dream." I always thank them for allowing me to live out my dream every day. Are some days hard? Absolutely! Are there days when I feel defeated? Absolutely! Am I exhausted? Absolutely! However, the good outweighs the bad. Are the smiles worth it? Absolutely! Are the light bulbs that turn on for the first time worth it? Absolutely! Is forming a relationship with a child that changes their perspective about school worth it? Absolutely! Is that one positive email from a parent worth it? Absolutely! In all of these scenarios, YOU as the teacher have the power to positively influence or impact someone else's life.

So, YOUR positivity is one of the most important tools you can have in your tool belt to impact students and learning. Starting with a greeting at the classroom door, YOUR attitude and energy reflects the environment YOU expect from your students.

DOI: 10.4324/9781003216988-89

Positive energy transfers to a supportive, safe, and encouraging classroom amongst yourself and your students. YOU have the ability to be that first agent of change. YOUR attitude sets the tone for the entire day and year.

YOUR attitude also helps form your relationships with students and colleagues that are a priority in getting students engaged and feeling confident. So, what are YOU going to do today to be that agent of change? YOU have the power to lift someone up with one smile, one laugh, one positive affirmation, etc. How will YOU share your positivity to impact students and learning? Be the positive agent of change. One word, one smile, one action at a time.

Sincerely,

YOUR BIGGEST FAN! :)
Kristi Kennedy

P.S.
As a new teacher, 25 years ago, there were times when I wanted to call it quits. I wanted to say I can't do this anymore. However, I remember my father (a retired teacher after 33 years) continued to remind me to focus on the positives of teaching and look for those positive moments that were the reason I chose teaching as a profession. The power of positivity is stronger than you think! YOU can make a difference!

The Lenses of Perspective

90

Dear Teacher,

We are considered "superhumans," individuals who possess "superpowers." I mean, what other profession has the skills to mold and shape the hearts, minds, and lives of children? Our "superpowers" complement each other. We have the POWER to be an encourager, nurturer, provider, problem-solver, storyteller, and artist. Mind you… all at the same time.

Let's face it: Superman has NOTHING on the teaching profession. Teacher, possessing all those qualities can either overwhelm you, allow you to grow tired and weary, or maybe have you second guess if you are in the right profession. These drawbacks can lead to negative thinking, lack of self-confidence, and the thoughts of "it's just a job." Allow me to encourage you with my little secret, a secret that will inspire you, especially when you have "one of those days." Anytime I second guess myself and I want to combat any negative thoughts, I put on my special lenses. Special lenses, you ask? Yes, special lenses. Because we are considered "superhumans," a teacher must possess a pair of special lenses. I call my special lenses, "The Lenses of Perspective." My lenses show me my why and allow me to reflect on my purpose, my reasons for becoming a teacher. When I put on my "The Lenses of Perspective", I am able to see that teaching is a part of who I am at my core. Teaching gives my heart a beat that sounds like laughter.

Teaching enables me to transform students' lives in a positive way. Teaching is the air I breathe. So, I say to you, Teacher, whenever you feel like you are not making an impact or feeling you are not doing enough, put on your special lenses and see what led you to become a teacher. Remember, there's a purpose

DOI: 10.4324/9781003216988-90

in everything. Look for it. Focus on your why. What's important is you are doing what you love and have amazing reasons for pursuing it.

Sarah Whitehead
Teacher in Washington

Thank You!

91

Dear Teacher,

Thank you for choosing to inspire, motivate, guide, comfort, encourage, and educate the eager minds who enter your classroom every day and light up at the sight of your face. You are their anchor. Regardless of what is going on elsewhere, once your students are in your presence, a weight is lifted, maybe not gone, but lifted because you are the beautiful soul who has provided a place of comfort for these children.

Thank you, teachers, for heading to school each morning, knowing there may be stacks of paperwork awaiting your attention, numerous meetings scheduled on your calendar, and distractions that you call, "not-teachable time," yet still ponder how blessed you are to have the opportunity to positively affect someone's life every day. What an AWESOME responsibility! Thank you for starting each day with a positive mindset, forgiving the stresses of yesterday, and beginning fresh because everyone needs and deserves a "Good Morning!" I know from experience that the way your day starts could very well indicate the way the day progresses all the way to the end of the day.

The best administrator I ever had the pleasure of working for would happily greet everyone with hugs, smiles, and high-fives every morning. One morning, when I was tardy, I walked into my classroom and he was in there. I prepared myself to be scolded, but instead he smiled and said, "Well, good morning Ms. Hutchings! We're so glad you made it to school safely today!" As my students cheered, my heart melted with gratitude and I knew at that moment that I would go above and beyond for this amazing leader. Therefore, teachers, thank you for having mercy on your tardy students. The majority of the time, it's not even the fault of the students who are tardy, especially if they don't drive themselves to school. The less of a scene you make of the tardy

DOI: 10.4324/9781003216988-91

and bigger deal you make of how glad you are that they made it to school, the more prepared the student will be to learn.

Thank you, teachers, for stopping mid-lesson when everything is flowing beautifully to give a student a Band-Aid without making them feel bad. I completely understand how frustrating it can be when a great lesson is interrupted, especially for a Band-Aid, but sometimes it's not really about that unnecessary adhesive strip covering a scab the student picked. Some kids just need a little extra care and attention, and that Band-Aid was a cloak of love and kindness from your heart, and thirty seconds later your lesson can continue flawlessly.

Thank you, teachers, for averting a crisis when something small, but huge to a child, occurs. Thank you for digging through your purse, enduring the pain of being stabbed by foreign objects, feeling sticky unknown substances, and wondering when the last time you cleaned out your purse was, just to find twenty-two cents at the bottom, so a student will have enough to buy the ice cream at lunch that she's been so excited about all morning. Of course, you know ice cream is extra, but she has her heart set on it, and she was only short by twenty-two cents. Your amazing sense of empathy has rewarded your student with the money to purchase the ice cream, as you are rewarded with the look of pure elation on the child's face as she chooses from the ice cream freezer during lunch. I guarantee that ice cream will be the best-tasting ice cream she ever eats!

Thank you, teachers, for giving Student X a question you know that he can answer correctly in front of the class, so he can feel proud and confident in front of his classmates. I know we've all had classes where academic levels may range from Kindergarten to Eighth Grade. That's where differentiation definitely comes in. One way to reach all students that some students may not admit to loving, but they secretly do, is by reading aloud to them. I am not kidding. It can be a picture book or part of a chapter book. Students love to relax and melt into another world for a few minutes. This also gives you, as the teacher, the opportunity to differentiate your questioning. Thus far, I have only taught as high as fifth grade, and I've never had a class that didn't LOVE for me to read to them. In today's virtual world, students still want to hear you, a human, their hero teacher, read live and lead their adventure.

Thank you, teachers, for taking the extra time when you get a chance to hand grade or write personal notes of praise and encouragement on students' papers before you hand them back as feedback. I know computers do the majority of scoring now, and they even have a place where you can type comments of praise if students choose the correct answer, but to me, that's not the same as a handwritten note from a teacher. If you do any kind of notes of praise, thank you! This truly means the world to students! Over the past twenty years, when I hand-graded endless stacks of papers, I'll admit it was very time-consuming, but worth it in the end. Not only did I love to put stickers on papers, but I loved to write notes of praise when students did very well because they deserved recognition for their hard work and effort. If a student was close to a high grade or scored in the average range, I'd write a note of encouragement and maybe provide some helpful hints.

This is the part, though, that touched my heart. If a student failed a paper, rather than writing something negative, which I would never do, nor would I ever give up on a child, I'd write on their paper about how much I believed in them and I how I understood that maybe that particular quiz/assignment was little harder or they didn't get a chance to study. I'd invite them to ask me any questions or see if they'd like to attend tutoring. The main point I'd emphasize was that I knew how smart they were. I believed in them and I couldn't wait to see their next paper. I'll never forget the notes they'd write back to me underneath my notes. They would thank me for believing in them and say they will do better next time. Then they would actually go on to pass the next assignment, maybe just barely, but that's still passing! I'd make a huge deal about it! Alone, I cried tears of joy.

Teachers, thank you for believing in all students. Everyone needs someone to believe in them. Thank you, teachers, for listening to your students' endless stories about topics that are important to them. Your therapeutic ear works wonders for their soul, and you may never truly know the difference you're making by simply listening, but your undivided attention is a blessing they may not receive anywhere else. Students need a trustworthy shoulder to cry on, an ear to listen to their deepest thoughts, a hand to hold when they are in doubt, and a heart to help carry their burdens. Thank you, teachers, for being that person for your students.

Thank you, teachers, for smiling and laughing with your class. When you tell jokes during a lesson, or allow a student to throw in a witty comment, and the classroom erupts into controlled laughter, an unseen bond of warmth flows throughout your classroom and connects everyone into a culture of comfort and trust. This is a debatable topic, but for me, laughter is one of the main ways my students and I related to each other, and I have always had strong bonds with my classes. My students thrived when I threw in funny anecdotes or witty comments throughout a lesson. In my collection of notes and letters from students, one of the most popular adjectives used to describe me was funny, then "humorous" because students wanted me to know they understood a better word for "funny". Thank you, teachers, for taking the time to make learning fun for your students.

Of course, there is the required content that must be taught, and sometimes even scripted curriculum, depending on where you teach, but when you can, thank you for finding ways to engage your students with video clips, songs, raps, hands-on activities, games, scavenger hunts, story books, or anything fun leading up to the topic you are about to teach. I also like to keep the fun going throughout the lesson and not just in the intro. I know this cannot happen all the time, but it certainly can when you want it to. I mentioned above how my students always described me in letters as being so funny, but more than that, almost every student on every academic level thanked me for always making learning fun! People always asked me why I stayed at school so late into the evenings. Many times I was grading papers or preparing lesson plans, but more times than not, I was creating fun activities to engage students in the lessons already prepared for that week. Teachers, students do realize how much work you put into these extra activities, especially the older the grade level. Thank you for sacrificing your time and using your creative gifts to provide the best education for your students.

Teachers, I must share this sweet story that demonstrates how much we mean to our students before I close. This story is part of my heart. When I began writing this letter, I intended to include excerpts from many of the letters I've collected from students over my 20 years of teaching so far (Yes, I've kept them all!). However, seeing that was an impossible task, I chose just one. I once taught a beautiful, intelligent little girl for both her 2nd grade and 4th grade year. She had a very rough home life, and school was her refuge. It broke my heart to see her cry any time she had to go home. Now teachers, please don't ever think you don't make a difference because this beautiful child wrote me a letter as fourth grader, first as her hero (which she won a contest for), and then a more personal letter with a picture of both of us at the bottom with giant teardrops falling from our eyes as we bid each other goodbye at the end of the year. Tears fall from my eyes as I type this part of her letter to me...

"Dear Ms. Hutchings,

You are the key to my heart and the key to my soul. I thank God for you every day. I am truly blessed to have you as my teacher. Thank you for making me who I am. I wouldn't be where I am now without you. You made me a smart, intelligent, loving person. You are too. I will never forget you, even when I retire. I love you dearly."

(I wish I could tell her, "You were always that amazing person. Thank you for making me a better teacher. I will always love you dearly.")

Most importantly, teachers, thank you for loving and caring for your students. Everything you do everyday with the students' best intentions in mind shines brightly.

You are true superheroes. I believe teachers are underpaid because the laborious, underappreciated work we do is priceless. There is not enough money to compensate someone who is a living angel to someone's child, equipping them with the loving care, knowledge, and skills to help make a better tomorrow. Contrary to what some may say, there are very few people who can stand in a teacher's shoes (especially heels), and serve students the way they are meant to be. Remember this, teachers, you will become a beautiful memory in all of your students' minds that will never fade; the memory of you will propel your former students to succeed. Thank you for creating a better tomorrow! Thank you for accepting this selfless calling because you were chosen to be a teacher.

Meghan Hutchings Meghan C. Hutchings
A Blessed Teacher in Texas

Moving from Surviving to Thriving

92

Dear Teacher,

For those individuals who have a genuine interest in helping young people develop, teaching can be a rewarding career. Over the course of my career, I have found that three things make the difference between happiness and frustration for a teacher. The star educator can effectively build relationships, is focused on students, and has effective organizational and time management skills.

Surprisingly, your ability to build relationships with your stakeholders, whether they are students, staff, or parents, impacts how well you perform as a teacher. For example, students who like and respect their teacher and classmates are less likely to exhibit behavior problems. Classrooms with a culture of mutual caring and respect are less dependent on "classroom management strategies" as a means of maintaining appropriate decorum.

Regardless of what grade or subject you teach, one of the most important things to remember is that your mission should be based on the concept "students–school–community." High-achieving schools have a mission of serving the students, school, and community to the best of their abilities. The teacher with a student-centered philosophy plans and teaches with the learner in mind. Carrying out guided reading is not a chore to the star teacher because he or she knows that the time spent in the small group will pay dividends in the future.

Finally, time management and organizational skills are crucial for any classroom or support teacher. Today's high-paced, high-demand education jobs require individuals who can manage a myriad of tasks successfully. You may have the best people skills and believe in helping young adults reach their fullest potential.

DOI: 10.4324/9781003216988-92

But how you organize your time will either make or break you. In addition, those educators with higher career aspirations can see those dreams crumble if they cannot set goals and manage time efficiently.

Garlfar Andrews
Assistant Principal in Dekalb County, GA

Take Time to Reach Them

93

Dear Teacher,

Have you ever wondered/questioned/reflected why you chose the teaching profession? I can honestly say that I never even gave it a thought in wondering or questioning, but sure continue to reflect on how to become better every day. I always knew that it was in me to be a teacher from a very young age; about five years old. My aunts (dad's sisters) were my first influence. They were avid readers and passed that on to me. I started reading (Spanish) at a very young age. By the time I started kindergarten at age six, I knew how to read and write. I was so advanced for kindergarten because I was reading everything I saw phonetically. My kindergarten teacher did not know what to do with me because I would not conform to sitting still and listen. I was distracted by anything that had words and was reading everything I saw. I was/am a passionate reader. So, I was placed in a 2nd grade classroom. Only problem was, I did not speak English and could not do the work. My 2nd grade experience lasted a month; I was moved back to kindergarten with the same teacher. Even though the kindergarten teacher looked like me, she would NOT speak Spanish to us. I was becoming so miserable and was beginning to hate school. I could not understand why a teacher that looked like me would not make the effort to help me learn and most of the other kids knew what was happening. At least that is what I saw.

Not soon after, we moved across the tracks and I had to change schools. We lived behind a Jr. high school and two blocks from my new elementary school: still a walking distance. My new kindergarten teacher, Ms. Hawkins, was different. Even though she did not speak Spanish herself, she took the time to teach and encouraged me to continue reading in Spanish. She gave me

DOI: 10.4324/9781003216988-93

English books to expand my reading library. This is when my LOVE of hoarding books began. She made EVERY effort to help me learn and ignited the LOVE of learning again. Mrs. Traylor (first grade), Mrs. Thomas (second grade), Mrs. Jackson (physical education) continued what Ms. Hawkins started; they made learning fun through play, art, music, and dance. To the point that I wanted to be like them. I took what I was learning at school home. I played school with neighborhood kids. I used to dumpster dive for books and supplies at the Jr. high school's dumpsters. It was a sight to see. I even made friends with the custodians from the school and sometimes they would gather supplies and walk over to drop them off at our front porch so that I would not get in trouble just in case the principal of the school or someone else would happen to see me in the dumpsters. Those were some GREAT memories – playing school with neighborhood kids. Just having fun till streetlights came on and time to head on home for the evening.

Like me, someone or something inspired you to become a teacher and become the second most valuable and important person in shaping a child's future; second because the child's parents/guardians are first. So, I leave you with some advice that has helped me throughout my years of teaching:

◆ Always give credit where credit is due. Thank those who inspired, motivated, and provided you with the resources be the best teacher that you are. In my case, my Franklin Elementary teachers Ms. Hawkins, Mrs. Traylor, Mrs. Thomas, Mrs. Jackson. Dr. Leigh VanHorn, UH-D professor, for guiding me and helping me see that my niche was in early childhood to 2nd grade age/group. Mrs. Carolyn Matthews for trusting my leadership abilities and pushing me into earning my master's degree in Curriculum and Instruction.

◆ Strive to being a lifelong learner. Continue doing your research and network with others in your grade level/subject, teachers outside your school/district, and your students. Here, I want to give special thanks to Sally Fowler Haughey, owner of Fairy Dust Teaching, for validating and expanding my knowledge in early childhood; introducing me to the unapologetic champion of play, Rae Pica; and guru of early childhood and neuroscience Dr. Mine Conkbayir.

◆ Build positive and meaningful relationship with whole school community. First and foremost, parents and students, including custodians, cafeteria staff, paraprofessionals, nurse, office staff, and secretary. Without them, we could not make learning and teaching possible. It takes a village to educate the whole child.

◆ Do not let others determine your students and your worth, be it administrators or standardized tests. You are the expert and professional in the classroom; you know your students' abilities, strengths, and needs. Own your profession, know your rights, and speak up when you must. For yourself, your students, and your peers.

◆ Most of all, make learning fun during normal school hours by embedding fine arts and play throughout ALL lessons, no matter the age, grade level or subject matter. Let students guide instruction and take ownership. You will be surprised what they have to offer.

On behalf of all students, parents, and fellow peers, thank you for choosing the teaching profession. Expect the unexpected and learn from the experience.

Isidro Rodriguez
Teacher in Texas

Be Creative

94

Dear Teacher,

You may be starting your first year, finishing up your last few years, or experiencing the beginning of burn out, somewhere in your career. Wherever you are in your teaching career, think of this year as an opportunity to be the most creative you have ever been. We make thousands of decisions every day, which results in a lot of successes and failures. Just remember to pay attention to the small successes throughout your day, even if it is just remembering to submit your attendance on time!

Teachers may not be the best students when we attend required staff meetings and professional development sessions, but we are dedicated to our own students and classrooms. Educators tend to be naturally curious and want to learn, so we may find ourselves reading books, articles, quotes and blogs, to find ideas, inspiration and insight. As I begin my 30th year of teaching, I find myself still inspired, passionate and ready to take on another school year, despite its unknown challenges. I find myself looking for the little things to keep me going.

When I first started teaching, I knew in my heart that teaching was for me. I loved the connections, the creativity and the freedom to touch lives through lessons and stories. I had a giant plan book, which held all of my whole language plans, now referred to as balanced literacy. I was able to teach thematic units, create my own time schedule for instruction and get lost in the art of teaching. I did not use the internet, copier or Zoom. We had a ditto machine, chalk and a filmstrip projector. I still remember having to check out the VCR/TV set up for special occasions.

On the first day of school, I was ready to take on these bright-eyed second graders and I knew it would go exactly as planned in my book! Well, I think it was lunch time when I felt the first urge to cry. I was walking my class of 28 second graders

DOI: 10.4324/9781003216988-94

down the hall and I was almost to the cafeteria with my line of students, when I heard the door to my room close. That's when I was overwhelmed with the thought of how large my class was, *how was I going to do this everyday? How was I going to be great at teaching, discipline, relationships and all of the other expectations now placed on me?*

I was one of two new teachers in this elementary school, and I was right out of college. Could you imagine being the only inexperienced teacher on your grade level? It is unheard of these days. To this day, I am so thankful that I had such a great support system. Just like my own teachers throughout my education, I remember the teachers on my grade level that were always there for me. We didn't have the opportunity to text or email; we took opportunities at lunch, recess and after school hours to talk. We supported each other, shared materials and funny stories, provided shoulders to cry on and advice for each other. We built strong connections with each other, in person.

One teacher specifically entertained me the most. She was my comic relief, a calm presence, and shared her wisdom freely. She will always be a part of my teaching heart. Irma was the one to tell me that everything in education will come full circle, just like the clothing styles, and she was right. As an experienced teacher of about 25 years, including taking time off to raise her boys, she had so many stories to tell. The most memorable was of her own experience, teaching in a one room school house. When I would question myself as a teacher, she used to pat my leg and say,"*Oh honey, you don't know how far education has come, I used to show up early to sweep the floors and get the fire started.*" I laughed the first time she told me, because I thought that she was kidding. She was not; she had started her career in a one room school house in North Carolina and had moved to Virginia, where she taught in a school with approximately six classrooms per grade level. I was amazed at her journey and her stories; I used to imagine the growth she had seen as she taught. I wondered if I would ever experience change like that.

I often wonder what she would say, watching us teach on Zoom.

I thought of Irma's one room school house a lot during the past year while I sat in my empty classroom and taught over Zoom. I spoke to my students on a screen, seeing a few faces daily, interacting with the few students who regularly participated online. I missed the controlled chaos, the noise and the interactions. I never could have imagined this situation when I first started teaching.

Fast forward to the present, and I find myself wondering how did I get here? There was no class in college to prepare me for this year. In a way, things were simplified when I first started teaching; the stress was different, but the expectations remain the same. To this day, educators are expected reach and teach our students, by any means possible. We need to be creative, engaging and effective. We hope the Wi-Fi connection is strong, the kids have their chargers and we are social distancing. We have less of an opportunity to connect in person and a high demand to connect through electronics.

We are expected to look out for our students and fellow teachers. Not only was I unsure how I was going to be successful throughout this past year, I often wondered, *How was I supposed to provide support to our new teachers, as a mentor?* I have been a mentor for most of my teaching career, and a mentor to multiple teachers in the last 15 years. I always try to provide the support that was given to me when I first became a teacher. I have learned so much from the new teachers that I have met throughout my career and I hope that they have taken little lessons from me with them. Mentoring is a great opportunity to teach and learn from each other. It's not good to be the smartest or most experienced person in the room; you always want to find an opportunity to grow and learn.

Being a teacher has become much more than just teaching a class. We are role models, mentors, entertainers, cheerleaders, friends, counselors, snack and supply providers, and so much more. We support the parents, families and community. We get up early, stay up late and work weekends, because we want to; it is our calling. We do it because we are passionate and we care.

Now is the time to build those connections. Reach out to your coworkers, create new relationships with the students and families. We must offer support, kind words and treats. Teachers, we've got this! We can do great things, together, inspiring each other, encouraging each other and cheering each other on.

Educators are the people who can have the most influence over a child. We create the climate in our classrooms; we control its weather. Just remember, you cannot have a rainbow without rain. Each day may be different, the winds can change at any time, but you have the opportunity to control what you bring to school each day; just don't forget your umbrella. I wish you the best of luck, you can do this.

Best Wishes,

Sara Silber
5th grade teacher

One Day at a Time

95

Dear Teacher,

We all have a different view on education whether we are elementary or secondary; whether we have our regular classroom students all day long or we send our students off every 25, 30, 45 or 50 minutes, they are all our students.

I have been a music educator for over 20 years. Either being greatly valued as a music teacher or treated as a glorified babysitter sets the tone for how productive I can be! Teach where you know you are valued and appreciated for your education and expertise.

Many professions view educators in so many different ways but always remember, we are the ones that make a difference and provide the foundation for the future. Teaching elementary music is the best! I believe in laying the foundation and being a strong foundation. Having my students come to me each time asking, "What are we doing today?" or "Can we do what we did last music time?" only shows me that they are enjoying what they are learning, and they want more of it. I have to enrich and supplement what I am teaching. That makes me a better teacher constantly!

As you are teaching your students, keep in mind a few important ideas; some of these may be already in use and some may be a helpful reminder:

*Active listening: as you are teaching your students to develop their listening skills, you are also helping them with the concept of active listening. The great part about this concept is we as teachers are also developing right along with our students! This is the intent to understand; effective communication which offers feedback or appropriate responses.

*Character: this is a developed skill over time. How we serve others or how we act when no one is watching. This skill

DOI: 10.4324/9781003216988-95

is definitely by example. I had a student teacher many years ago call me out on this. I was not aware that I was even modeling this for my students because it is part of me, it's engrained in me. When you go into this profession, have the mindset of humility – a servant's heart. Develop into the person we long to be and these character traits will come through our teaching, the way we interact with our students and our fellow teachers. Have the mindset of being selfless, expecting nothing in return. When you have a willing heart to be the best version of yourself, for your students and staff it will show in everything you do and say.

Teaching is a profession that no teacher experiences the same way. Rely on each other to be there for one another. Share experiences, listen to each other. Some of your closest friends will be teachers because you have experiences that no one else will ever understand.

My teaching experiences have been in rural and urban settings. These are night and day differences, but the friendships were genuine because we were with each other, supporting one another through the good and the bad. You are not alone. Be sure to reach out to other teachers and let them know you are there.

Have a great school year! Take it one day at a time... sometimes one hour at a time. That is OK! Remember you have the privilege to educate tomorrow's future.

Debbie Merriman
Music Educator

Never Stop Believing 96

Dear Teacher,

The lives that are created and touched by a teacher's heart are far more than one can count. The job description requires more than a preferred degree of study, instructional planning or the outline of a curriculum; it is designed by the matters of the heart. Students are not one size fits all and unfortunately, they are not packaged with an instruction guide. However, the truth of the matter is they are developed and molded based upon experiences. Reflecting over the years that I served as a classroom teacher, I felt that I was more of a change agent for at least two or more students on a daily basis.

Many students that I taught attended rural schools or Title I schools. According to the demographics, the statistical data would most often highlight the low ranking of test scores on state assessments, 100% of the students receiving free and reduced lunch, the high poverty rate and the shortage of teachers. Often, I would find myself asking the same questions over and over again in almost every data meeting, Is it about demographics? Is it truly only about benchmarking? Is it really about the lack of parental engagement? These are the questions that would always bring me back to the matters of the heart.

You have to know that when it comes to addressing the matters of one's heart, it goes through a process that includes three components: validation, hope, and belief. Validation for most students is defined as the need to feel that they are part of or belong. Never forget that many students will come to you displaced, from broken homes, motherless, fatherless, with regret, fearful and confused. They will show up to school each day seeking validation beyond the brick and mortar that they are important. They will seek validation that says they are more than a grade of an A, B, C, D or F. They will continue to show

DOI: 10.4324/9781003216988-96

up each day to gauge their own personal level of validity based upon how you speak to them, acknowledge their presence and interact with them.

Hope for most students is defined as an inner emotion of a state of being. They hope that they have what it takes to make the difference for their families and to personally succeed. They will show up hoping that no one is able to determine that he or she didn't rest well the night before due to the power being off and they were either too cold or too hot. They will show up hoping that they are able to clean up the cafeteria after the last lunch wave in order to take home a doggy sack just to ensure that they will dinner for the night. They will show up hoping that the after school or extended school program lasts each day of the week because they don't look forward to going home to an abusive parent or indecent home life. They are simply trying to find their way.

As you go throughout your teaching career, you will be reminded that because you believed in a child, they have succeeded. It is going to take you believing in them while they are not able to see past the present struggles with a constant cycle of molding their minds and heart with love. Belief is defined as inner strength needed to face adversity. On your hardest days, I want you to think about the person who has influenced you the most. The person that believed in you. If you have a hard time remembering or have brain freeze during that moment, remember that you have an entire classroom of past and present little people who believe in you. They believe in your smiles, encouragement, hard work, small talks, hard talks, private and whole group advice, teaching style and your ability to continue to lead them in the right direction.

Teaching is not for the faint at heart and oftentimes it inflicts a lot of stress and frustration on you throughout various times in your career. However, remember that because of you, a student will become a doctor, a lawyer, a judge, a teacher, a good parent, a pastor, and so many more things. You are making a difference in every student's life that enters your classroom door. I'm a firm believer that things do not occur based upon happenstance. You are where you are supposed to be, you're doing exactly what you were destined and you are making a much bigger impact than you will ever know. Don't doubt your progress, don't become bitter or upset if you don't have the highest test scores in the school or if your homeroom class has the highest attendance rates; remember that if the matters of the heart are addressed then all things will fall in place. Never stop believing.

Kelia Burns-Browder, Ed.S.
Principal

Encouragement from a Veteran Teacher

Dear Teacher,

As a veteran educator entering my twenty-fifth year of teaching, there have been quite a few affirmational moments in my career; however, there are two instances that are paramount and to which I attribute the fact that I am still teaching – with just as much passion and commitment as my first year. One actually occurred before my teaching career truly began, as it was during my student teaching experience. I was very blessed to be placed with two phenomenal and experienced teachers during my internship. As I was leaving the school one afternoon carrying many papers that needed to be graded and lessons that needed further planning, my mentor teacher told me a story of when she was a first year teacher, leaving her school in the same manner as me – arms heavy with papers and books. She explained that her principal stopped her, took all of those papers and books, and sent her home without them. He explained to this young teacher that while grading papers and planning lessons is important and essential, it is also important and essential to take care of yourself. I have always felt fortunate that my mentor teacher chose to impart this same wisdom to me. *As a teacher, it is inevitable that you will devote some of your time at home completing things for work; however, there has to be a balance between your work life and your personal life. If you take work home all the time,* you will find yourself in a position that is not sustainable. I have tried to apply this sage advice throughout my career and firmly credit that little nugget of wisdom to my longevity as a teacher.

The second affirmational moment came to me as a realization through talking (and honestly commiserating at times) with my colleagues. Educators are not always given the recognition and credit we so deserve. This recognition may not come from

DOI: 10.4324/9781003216988-97

your colleagues, your leadership team, or our society. As a result, sometimes you have to realize your worth as an educator does not come from these outside sources, but instead, it comes from within the four walls of your classroom. It comes from those students who visit your classroom after school for a listening ear; it comes from students who come back to visit you after they are no longer in your class because of the impact you had on their lives; it comes from those students who seek you out on social media years after they graduate to let you know of your influence; it comes from students who become educators and look to you for guidance on managing their own classrooms. These are the best forms of recognition, and in my opinion, they are far more memorable and impactful than any credit I could receive from those who remain outside of my classroom. So, when you doubt your self-worth as an educator, think about the affirmations you receive from within those four walls of your classroom. They are the ones that demonstrate the most.

Sincerely,

Holly Ramey Chatham
English Teacher

The "Ideal" Student 98

Dear Teacher,

A few years ago, I had a student that I would call the ideal student. He always completed his work on time, never caused a disruption, and if you asked him to do something, he did it. He was the type of student that we all wish we could fill our classrooms with. As I observed him more, I realized he rarely talked to any of his classmates, really kept to himself, and honestly... I concluded that I really didn't know a lot about him. One day during class, I asked him to meet me during Quality Time (a 10–15-minute check-in time). We sat down and we just talked. From that one meeting, we ended up meeting 2–3 times a week for months. We talked about everything from his homelife, his fears, his goals after high school, his interests, and the list goes on and on.

In the beginning I steered clear of discussing his progress in my class because my sole focus was to get to know him at a deeper level. I knew how he was performing in my class, I didn't need to ask him that. This quiet, ideal student was struggling with things I never imagined he was struggling with. I wouldn't have known about these internal struggles had I not taken the time to get to know him. This was about three years ago. Two years ago I left my position at that school and moved to a different district. On my last day at the school, I got a letter from him thanking me for being the one person in the building that took the time to get to know him and build a real relationship with him. A few months ago I got an email from him thanking me for reaching out and helping him. Two years have passed since he gave me the letter on my last day and his last email; and to be honest, I didn't realize that my small investment had such a large impact on this student!

If you don't think students won't remember you, you're wrong. How do you want to be remembered? I encourage you to take the time to build real, authentic relationships with your

DOI: 10.4324/9781003216988-98

students. They may not always tell you, but those words, those moments, and the time you invested can make a real difference. I thought about the type of leader I wanted as an educator and realized that this was the type of educator I needed to be:

- ◆ Want a leader that will inspire you? Inspire your students.
- ◆ Want a leader that will listen to you? Listen to your students.
- ◆ Want a leader that will check in with you? Check in with your students.
- ◆ Want a leader that will be empathetic, kind, and show you grace? Show your students empathy, kindness, and grace.

If making an impact drives your purpose, then your purpose will make an impact. Never underestimate the power of true, authentic connections and never underestimate your ability to make a difference. Every student deserves to have someone in their corner and I challenge you to be that person. It is easy to build those connections with the outgoing and friendly students and it's easy to recognize a cry for help through behaviors, but don't forget to seek out those "ideal" students that may have struggles that you don't know anything about. You got this!

Mrs. Allison Stansberry
6–12 Principal, Raymond Central Public School

Find Your S.H.I.N.E.   99

Dear Edustar,

You are a gift. Yes, you. You are a gift to those who need you as YOU stepped up to the plate. Don't second guess that. Don't second guess you. It's easy for us to find and see the flaws we have. We've been trained to do so. Society has "raised us" to often look for what we need to improve, work on or even be. In the process, we lose the *Lion of Greatness* (what you were born with and developed who you are)! When looking in the mirror, who do you see? Do you see the confident educator (the Lion(ess) of Greatness) or the educator who thinks they need to continue to improve... just not good enough? Before you completely decide, read on.

There are traps to avoid in our world and in education. They impact us personally and they impact us professionally.

Trap #1: The Comparison Trap

Education is not immune to the comparison game. We have the peer next door, or in another school building, to whom we could pull out an arbitrary measuring stick and compare the engagement they foster, the creative lessons they impart, the behavior issues they manage to resolve, every committee on which they serve, and the list goes on and on. If you want to compare to push yourself to be a bit better and better or to self-reflect so you can grow in confidence, that's fine. But if you are doing so in a way that is knocking you down and causing you to guess where your heart is, then you are playing the Comparison Game... a game that an Edustar like you does NOT play. They are not you and you are not them.

DOI: 10.4324/9781003216988-99

Trap #2: You are "Average"

You are not average. You are an Edustar! So many times we down-play who we are out of concern for appearing braggadocious or that it draws attention to ourselves, opening us up to being judged. Consequently we pull back on what we have to offer. Guess what? You weren't meant to play small and people will always judge you anyway. Keep in mind that judging from a nega-tive lens is often done from people who feel less than average or maybe even "just" average. When we step into who we are, we acknowledge what we ARE good at doing! You aren't saying you are good at everything, but rather acknowledging your strengths and gifts that you have to offer. When you lift yourself up to share your strengths you serve others at a high level. And when you sprinkle in the passion for what you are doing, then there is no way you are average. Imagine others doing the same! That is the world I want to live in. One where we embrace who we are and embrace it so we can add value, serve, and contribute posi-tively to the world. You are going to be average on some things and less than average on others. That. Is. Okay. Welcome to being human! We work on improving – always – but let's not forgot the greatness that you have to support others and enrich their life.

If you have lost your S.H.I.N.E. or are needing to bring that light within you to an illuminating level, then consider these five tips.

S.elf – Allow your strengths to serve you and serve others. Create a list and ask friends what are the greatest skills you have that make their life better.

H.eart – Explore your passions – those things that bring you energy, put a smile on your face, or make you lose track of time. Embed more of those in your life.

I.nspire – Music, quotes, artwork, people, objects… the list goes on. Identify what brings you that momentum to keep going and keep them nearby for those times of need or to make sure you sprinkle them in daily or weekly.

N.avigate – Create a plan of action to put your strengths, passions and inspiration into your daily life. Highlighting this about you brings an awareness that then allows you to implement these moments and things so that you can see more of how you illuminate those around you. Including you!

Exceptional – Look in the mirror at the end of the day and be proud of who you are. Forget all the policies or standards that don't serve our students. Make the choice to do what is best for students that is within your control and you will have made a difference in the lives of others. Man that feels good!

No one could have imagined all the things we would deal with in our lifetime. The way educators have had to shift how they teach and where they teach. The way the world would stop due to a global pandemic. The way exhaustion would set in like never before. Yet, here you are! Reading this uplifting book of support for YOU. A book that reminds you that you are not alone.

I say that again, you are not alone.

I stand with you.

With hugs,

Lavonna Roth
Creator of Ignite your Shine

Empath Fatigue

100

Dear Teacher,

Teachers are some of the most caring, affirmational, and kind people on earth. This is one reason teachers are so important to students and to society in general, because they give their all for their students. But it is also one of the reasons that teachers experience burnout and why there is such a high attrition rate in education as well. I have been fortunate to travel the country and talk with thousands of educators over the past several years. But if there is one attribute of teachers that seems to surface in conversations it is something called empath fatigue.

Empath fatigue is a type of stress that comes from helping people day in and day out. It occurs when someone cares too much about too many people and becomes emotionally depleted.

The stress and hardship of what you're experiencing, seeing and feeling starts to take a toll on you. Think about it, as a teacher you often feel the pain and struggles of your students and often even carry that home with you in the evenings. It is part of what makes you a great teacher, but it is also what can cause you to be overwhelmed, fatigued, exhausted and just burnt out.

To help you with empath fatigue get in the habit of asking yourself these five questions to reflect on for your own well-being:

- is it my stress or other people's stuff?
- am I empowering or enabling?
- am I sacrificing too much?
- is my sense of purpose realistic or superhero level?
- am I self caring?

As you can see from the questions, we are guilty of adding to our fatigue by taking on too much, sacrificing too much, and

DOI: 10.4324/9781003216988-100

ignoring our own self-care. Below is a list of strategies to help you prevent or at least manage empath fatigue.

1. **Focus on self-care**.
   ◆ Balanced, nutritious diet
   ◆ Regular exercise
   ◆ Routine schedule of restful sleep
   ◆ Indulge in self occasionally, such as pedicure, massage, night out with friends.
2. **Set emotional boundaries**. Separate what you wish you could do from what you know you can do. You may feel that you are not doing enough—a sure way of developing stress and feeling overwhelmed.
3. **Balance work and home life**. When all your time is spent working or thinking about work, it can be easy to burn out. Work–life balance is important and making time for leisure activities and personal hobbies outside of work can help lower stress levels and improve overall life satisfaction
4. **Show gratitude**. Gratitude is all about mindset. Don't just feel gratitude, express it! Let your class, colleagues, and administration know you are grateful for them. But also show this gratitude with your family and friends as well.

Teaching is one of the hardest jobs in the world. It can be physically and emotionally depleting. And these past couple of years have made it all but unbearable. When you combine that with the fact that most teachers speak an affirmational language and have empath qualities, it is no wonder teachers are burned out. But hopefully you can recognize the signs of empath fatigue and focus on the four areas discussed to help you lighten your emotional burden that teachers carry. Along with all the uplifting letters from your fellow educators, you can find a healthy balance and maintain your sanity and your joy of teaching! Because while teaching may be one of the toughest jobs, it is also one of the most rewarding jobs, and you do impact the lives of all the students you teach. So, take care of yourself, so you can be at your best, to give your best, to make a positive difference in their lives. Thank you all for the amazing work you do in preparing our children for the future!

Dr. Brad Johnson
(Author of *Dear Teacher*)

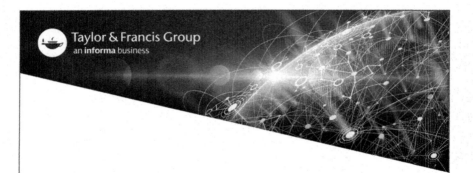